Reform by Numbers

Reform by Numbers

Measurement Applied to Customs and Tax Administrations in Developing Countries

Thomas Cantens, Robert Ireland, and Gaël Raballand
Editors

THE WORLD BANK
Washington, D.C.

ISBN (paper): 978-0-8213-9713-8
ISBN (electronic): 978-0-8213-9714-5
DOI: 10.1596/978-0-8213-9713-8

Cover image and design: Naylor Design, Inc.

Library of Congress Cataloging-in-Publication Data

Reform by numbers: measurement applied to customs and tax administrations in developing countries/ edited by Thomas Cantens, Robert Ireland, Gaël Raballand.
    p. cm.
  Includes bibliographical references.
  ISBN 978-0-8213-9713-8 — ISBN 978-0-8213-9714-5 (electronic)
  1. Customs administration—Developing countries. 2. Taxation—Developing countries. 3. Tax administration and procedure—Developing countries. I. Cantens, Thomas. II. Ireland, Robert. III. Raballand, Gaël. IV. World Bank.
  HJ7390.R44 2012
  352.4'4091724—dc23   2012031325

Contents

Tables

Foreword

The word *reform* is a constant in the daily life of a customs officer. No customs administration among the 177 members of the World Customs Organization has not had a reform program in progress or planned. This is ultimately quite normal. Contrary to the widespread notion that states have entered a new and onerous cycle of perpetual reform in recent years, reform has always been a core characteristic of administrative life. Moreover, as its mission evolves over the years, a customs administration inevitably has to embrace reform to better respond to the challenges posed by its ever-changing environment. Indeed, reform is the dynamic of the state, especially when it crosses topics as political and technical as revenue and border management. In developing countries, where the state remains one of the major organizers of the society, the administrative dynamics appear more difficult to perceive because they are modestly publicized and often judged against expectations raised or defined externally. The evaluation of administrations that have conducted reforms is often judged by a comparison with ideal models of bureaucracy and standards—often without adequate regard to their environment and necessary developmental phases; in contrast, change is always the result of an addition of slow and empirical processes, best achieved when driven by an ownership approach. Consequently, time must be given to reforms as long as reformers are able to demonstrate that positive changes are happening. When changes do not meet the initial objectives, customs managers should, when appropriate, seek improvements other than what was originally expected. To achieve this goal, reformers must know how to decipher the change, understand its variations, and capture its effects. Accordingly, new and innovative reform strategies are needed. One approach that is currently garnering respect and attention is the use of measurement.

Numbers are the universal language that can reconcile aspirations for reform, discourses, and actions. Quantifying is more than recording and presenting. Figures reflect an intelligible and neutral understanding about what is happening on the ground. These benefits are frequently unknown or unavailable to policy makers and donors: measurement can alleviate this lack of data by clarifying the confusing representations and understandings between professional communities and making the efficiency of administrative procedures and their evolution easier to appreciate.

Measurement is therefore equivalent to marking what has changed amid what may seem to be continuing failures and inertia. Thus, quantification is courageous because it challenges simple slogans and identifies reality. As such, I welcome the initiatives of the Algerian, Cameroonian, Korean, French, and Senegalese customs administrations, whose experiences are described in this book. They show how measurement reveals their failures as well as their successes, which feeds internal debates on preferred methods of reform based on evidence. These exercises in transparency can become a principle of governance adopted by the whole customs community. This book is thus an opportunity for experts from international institutions that work with customs in developing countries to develop new forms of dialogue and cooperation on both the objectives of reform and the means of their achievement.

Kunio Mikuriya, Secretary General
World Customs Organization

Acknowledgments

The editors thank the authors for their valuable contributions to this book: Guillermo Arenas, Hanane Benyagoub, Samson Bilangna, Aissa Boudergui, Ousmane Coundoul, Marcellin Djeuwo, Massène Gadiaga, Anne-Marie Geourjon, Bertrand Laporte, José-María Muñoz, Hakim Nait Abdelselam, Xavier Pascual, and Soyoung Yang.

The book benefited from additional contributions by Chang-Ryung Han and Patricia Revesz. Bernard Hoekman provided overall guidance.

Najy Benhassine, Paul Brenton, and Enrique Fanta reviewed book chapters.

Publication Professionals LLC copyedited the book.

The editors thank participants of the WCO–World Bank–Algeria Customs Research Conference on Measurement in Customs and Tax Administrations in Developing and Emerging Countries, held in March 2012, especially Kunio Mikuriya, secretary general of the World Customs Organization, and Abdelkerim Djoudi, minister of finance of Algeria, who opened the conference. They are grateful to Mohamed Abdou Bouderbala, the head of the Algerian customs administration, who made this event possible and successful, and Mohammed Benguerna, Giorgio Blundo, Mohamed Yassine Ferfera, and Fouzi Mourji, who agreed to engage in dialogue with the authors and conduct the debates during the conference. The editors also thank Saïd Bensalem, Hocine Bouzid,

Souhila Hammouche, Hacène Himeur, Fatma-Zohra Lounici, and Mohamed Talaïlef from the Algerian customs administration, whose hard work made the conference a fertile working environment. In addition, the editors thank Djoudi Rachid Zitouni and the Algerian Ministry of Culture for their special contributions to make the conference a pleasant moment for all participants.

Finally, the editors thank the Algerian customs administration, the Islamic Development Bank, the customs administration of the Republic of Korea, and the French customs administration for providing funding for the Algiers workshop. They thank the Cameroon World Bank office, especially Greg Binkert and Cia Sjetnan, for publishing the book; the Trade Facilitation Facility for financing the experiment with Cameroon Customs; Madeleine Chungkong; and Stephen McGroarty and Stephen Pazdan from the World Bank Office of the Publisher, for their assistance during the book publication process.

About the Contributors

Guillermo Arenas is an economist with a master's degree in public administration from the Maxwell School of Citizenship and Public Affairs from Syracuse University (New York). He is currently a consultant with the World Bank's International Trade Department.

Hanane Benyagoub is currently the head of the Public Relations and Information Division at the Algerian customs administration. After studying to become a lawyer, she obtained a master's degree in criminal law and criminology and a master's degree in strategic studies and international policy. She is now a PhD student in criminal law at Algiers University.

Samson Bilangna was the head of the Information Technology Department of Cameroon Customs. He is now a technical officer at the World Customs Organization Headquarters, working, among other things, on the Time Release Study and the Revised Kyoto Convention.

Aissa Boudergui is the head of the Regional Direction of Algiers port. He graduated from the National School of Administration and will soon defend his PhD in economics at Algiers University.

Thomas Cantens is an anthropologist, member of the Research and Strategies Unit of the World Customs Organization, and researcher at the Centre Norbert Elias–École des Hautes Études en Sciences Sociales (France).

Ousmane Coundoul is a member of the Risk Analysis and Decision Support Unit of Senegalese Customs.

Marcellin Djeuwo is the head of the Risk Analysis Unit of Cameroon Customs.

Massène Gadiaga is a member of the Risk Analysis and Decision Support Unit of Senegalese Customs.

Anne-Marie Geourjon was a senior lecturer in economics from Université d'Auvergne (France). She is currently a senior fellow at the Fondation pour les Études et Recherches sur le Développement International and an associate researcher at the Centre d'Études et de Recherches sur le Développement International.

Robert Ireland is a policy analyst. He heads the Research and Strategies Unit of the World Customs Organization.

Bertrand Laporte is a senior lecturer in economics at the Université d'Auvergne (France) and a researcher in the Centre d'Études et de Recherches sur le Développement International. He cochairs a master's program specialized in public finance in emerging and developing countries.

José-María Muñoz is an anthropologist. He was a postdoctoral fellow in the Emory Program in Development Studies, Emory University, Atlanta, and is now lecturer at the University of Edinburgh's Centre of African Studies.

Hakim Nait Abdelselam is a senior inspector at the Judicial Studies Department of the Algerian customs administration. He graduated from the National School of Administration and is a master's student in international affairs at Algiers University.

Xavier Pascual is the deputy head of the Internal Audit Unit of French Customs, in charge of performance policy.

Gaël Raballand is a senior public sector specialist in the World Bank's Middle East and North Africa region.

Soyoung Yang is the deputy director of the Korea Customs Service.

Abbreviations

ASP	application service providing (system)
ASYCUDA	Automated System for Customs Data
AWB/S	air waybill slip
BAD	*Bureau d'Analyse et d'Aide à la Décision*, or Analysis and Decision-Making Support Bureau (Senegal)
BPR	business process reengineering
CCG	*Cellule de contrôle de gestion*, or Management Control Unit (France)
CFAF	*Communauté Financière Africaine francs*, or African Financial Community francs
CIF	cost, insurance, and freight
CITES	Convention on International Trade in Endangered Species of Wild Fauna and Flora
CREAD	*Centre de Recherche en Économie Appliqué pour le Développement*, or Applied Development Economics Research Centre (Algeria)
DA	*Dinar Algérien* (Algerian currency)
DGE	*Direction des Grandes Entreprises*, or Large Business Office (Cameroon)
DGI	*Direction Générale des Impôts*, or Directorate General of Taxation (Cameroon)

DPI	declaration prior to import
DPO	*direction par objectifs*, or management by objectives
DPPO	*direction participative par objectifs*, or participatory management by objectives
EU	European Union
EU-27	27 member states of the European Union
FOB	free on board
GDP	gross domestic product
HS	Harmonized System
ISP	information strategic planning
KCS	Korea Customs Service
KRW	Korean won
LOLF	*Loi organique relative aux lois de finances*, or Constitutional Bylaw on Budget Acts (France)
MBO	management by objectives (theory)
NPM	new public management (theory)
OECD	Organisation for Economic Co-operation and Development
PINORAC	*Projet d'Introduction des Normes de Rendement dans l'Administration Camerounaise*, or Project for the Introduction of Performance Standards (Cameroon)
PROMAGAR	*Promotion de la Gestion Axée sur les Résultats*, or Program for the Modernization of the Administration through Performance-Based Management (Cameroon)
PVI	*programme de vérification des importations*, or import verification program
RCT	randomized control trial
SAGAR	*Système Automatisé de Gestion et d'Analyse de Risque*, or Automatic Risk Management and Analysis System (Senegal)
SAR	Special Administrative Region (China)
SIAR	*Système Informatisé d'Analyse de Risque*, or Computerized Risk Analysis System (Senegal)
SIGAD	*Système Informatique de Gestion Automatisé des Douanes*, or Automated Customs Management Information System (Algeria)
SIGCD	*Système d'Information de Gestion du Contentieux Douanier*, or Information System to Manage Customs Litigation (Algeria)

SIGIPES	*Système Informatique de Gestion Intégrée des Personnels de l'État et de la Solde,* or Computer System for the Integrated Management of State Personnel and Payroll (Cameroon)
SWL	single window lite
SYDAM	*Système de Dédouanement Automatisé des Marchandises,* or Automated System for Customs Clearance of Goods
TFSW	trade facilitation single window
UN Comtrade	United Nations Commodity Trade Statistics Database
VAN	value-added network
West AFRITAC	West Africa Regional Technical Assistance Center (International Monetary Fund)
WITS	World Integrated Trade Solution (software)

CHAPTER 1

Introduction

Thomas Cantens, Robert Ireland, and Gaël Raballand

In his book *Le vocabulaire des institutions indo-européennes* (1969), later published in English as *Indo-European Language and Society* (1973), Émile Benveniste, a French linguist, raises an insightful point. The Latin word *duco* and Greek word *hēgéomai* have the same meaning and evolution: in the literal sense, they mean "to lead, to command," and they evolved to a figurative sense meaning "to judge, to estimate." At least for the Latin, Benveniste found the bridge between literal and figurative senses: computing, calculation. In classical Latin, one used to "draw up an account" by writing and calculating from the bottom to the top of numbers series. Benveniste (1969, 152) writes:[1]

> Through the mediation of an expression where *ducere* signifies "to bring an account to its total" (*rationem ducere*), hence "count," we can understand the phrase *aliquid honori ducere* "to count something as honorable," or *aliquem honestum ducere* "to count somebody as honorable." It is always the idea of "to make a total." The conditions determining the specialization of sense were thus produced by the technique of computing.

Leading and estimating were, thus, linked through numbers. Several centuries later, this linguistic bridge between leading and estimating is still the core of the reflections that are discussed in this book: how measurement is used to lead reforms in customs and tax authorities.

National policy makers and international organizations have applied a variety of strategies to reform customs and tax administration in developing countries. Donors, such as the World Bank and the International Monetary Fund, and intergovernmental organizations, such as the World Trade Organization and the World Customs Organization, are active in providing development assistance. Many public institutions in developing countries have benefited from this assistance. Debates continue, however, about which development methods are helpful and which are not—or are possibly even harmful. Some customs and tax administrations that have embarked on ambitious reforms have made little progress, which results in an inability to raise markedly their effectiveness and efficiency. Moreover, corruption and vested interests frequently block reform.

A key problem faced by customs and tax authorities in their reform policies is that the use of accurate material and verifiable evidence has been inadequate. Without valid problem identification, improvement techniques cannot be devised. Moreover, with respect to development assistance, there has been an overreliance on measuring *inputs* rather than *impact* (Bigsten, Gunning, and Tarp 2006). This collective book contends that innovative approaches should be introduced or expanded with the objective of successfully reforming customs and tax functions.

Informed information gathering and analysis through measurement and experiment can produce incentivization; reductions in information asymmetry; and depoliticization of knowledge in customs and tax reform, capacity building,[2] and modernization. *Incentivization* means motivating individuals and collectives to improve their behavior and productivity on the basis of numbers. *Reduction in information asymmetry* is essentially the principal-agent problem: managers and operational staff members do not share the same reality because they have differing access to information. *Depoliticization of knowledge* entails eliminating the creation or use of subjective and invalid information. Public policy debate and decisions are frequently influenced by ill-informed opinion rather than by research and evidence. A marked shift is needed from inaccurate conventional wisdom or unproven shibboleths to models that are tested in the field. A crucial part of this effort is more emphasis on empiricism and measurement of tangible realities. The central reason to emphasize the use of numerical quantification that is as objective and accurate as possible is to improve decision making. Evidence, of course, must then be communicated widely to raise awareness.

Small experiments that test ideas should also be tried more often. We do not contend that measurement is the only solution, and we would be disappointed if it was the only one applied, but measurement is a reform strategy that bears more attention and emphasis. In particular, we advocate the deployment of appropriate measurement strategies into customs and tax authority reforms in developing countries.

Focus on measurement also brings an important debate to the surface: whether reform should take a holistic approach or whether gradual, focused reform is preferable. The *holistic reform model* demands strategic planning that simultaneously confers equal importance on every key administrative element, including infrastructure, legislation, management, personnel, funding, procedures, corruption, and technology. The *gradual, focused reform model* demands that a customs administration pinpoints one or a few core deficiencies and aggressively pursues their amelioration. Although the holistic model should not be discounted, we worry that it is inflexible and can lead to inertia. For instance, if an administration defers concrete reform steps pending adjustments to legislation, it may wait a very long time. This inertia may delay relatively easier but higher-impact changes.

Finally, as Rajaram, Raballand, and Palale (2010) state, "Reforming public sector requires a change in behavior and mindsets of people; cars, computers and formal training do not help in most cases." Performance measurement experiments demonstrate the importance of individual incentives and of staff policies, which are nevertheless usually neglected in donor-financed programs because they are difficult to implement and are socially and politically sensitive. There is a need to assess and change *individual* performance, which is different from revenue targets.

This book includes chapters that describe several examples of where measurement was used during reform programs.

The Importance of Performance Measurement in Customs and Tax Administrations

Two main features characterize taxation in developing countries:

- Tax effort is lower than in developed countries: less than 20 percent of gross domestic product (GDP) compared with 30 percent of GDP in Organisation for Economic Co-operation and Development (OECD) countries.
- The share of customs revenues and trade-related taxes is high: 25–70 percent of total budget revenues, oil revenues excluded.

Tax collection efficiency is therefore important, because revenues are usually low and depend on trade-related taxes.

Quantified and comparative measurement of performance appeared in the 1970s when the new public management (NPM) theory emerged. NPM recommendations are still being discussed theoretically and empirically and have contributed to pressure from donors for development results on the ground.

According to literature in this area, measurement is used in public service for many reasons. Without necessarily endorsing them all, Behn (2003) suggests that public managers have eight broad purposes for measuring performance: evaluate, control, budget, motivate, promote, celebrate, learn, and improve.

The central purpose for using measurement or any other technique in customs and tax reform should be to help an agency improve its *effectiveness* while optimizing its *efficiency*. For tax authorities, *effectiveness* means collecting to the extent possible the amount of revenue that is due according to the tax base and rates. With respect to customs authorities in developing countries, the key objective is also raising the appropriate amount of customs duties and taxes based on the volume and types of goods crossing the country's border and the existing tariff rates.[3]

The revenue raised by customs and tax authorities is used ideally to fund public services such as transport infrastructure, health care, defense, law enforcement, and education. If one considers an extended continuum of revenue collection effectiveness, how the public funds are spent is ultimately a consideration for the society as a whole. If the populace views government-collected revenue as being misspent or squandered, it can negatively impact compliance rates and thus the effectiveness of customs and tax administrations.

The *efficiency* of border procedures, which is known as *trade facilitation* in customs jargon, is also growing in discourse popularity in developing countries. Trade facilitation entails simplifying border regulatory controls to reduce unnecessary impositions on traders while recognizing that some customs controls are necessary and mandated by policy makers. A variety of factors affect efficiency in border controls, including the quantity and quality of border officers, whether automation and risk management (selectivity) are used, the complexity of goods classification and valuation, the number of documents required, and the amount of duplication caused by multiplicity of border agencies. Ultimately, trade facilitation is measured by trade transaction costs and the length of dwell times of goods at borders.

Measurement or quantification can assist in transforming the unknown into the known and opinion into fact. Reasoned performance indicators can be turned into objective data as a basis on which to analyze and draw conclusions. This approach implies not only identifying what the object to be measured is (for example, an agency, an agency's employee or employees, a procedure, a problem, or a program) but also defining both upstream what value is attached to an indicator (for example, distinguishing between the less than average, the average, and the more than average) and downstream what is to be done following the measurement (what decision is made).

Measurement can foster better relations within public administration between colleagues and between an administration and its external stakeholders (political masters, users, and donors). When one is seeking to achieve an optimal level of revenue, improve the effectiveness of controls, enhance trade facilitation, strengthen political authority and internal control, or improve relations with different types of users, measurement is an administrative technique that furthers objectivity.

Taxation is considered as a way to increase public demand for more government accountability, which contributes to state-building processes and creates a fiscal social contract (IDS 2010; Moore 2007). Formalizing this view, measurement in customs and tax administrations is fundamental to enable the state to make accountability possible and publicize its own results, whether they concern revenue collection, controls legitimacy, or public expenditure.

Ease of Performance Measurement in Customs and Tax Administrations

Paradoxically as it may seem; performance measurement is easier in customs and tax administrations than in many other areas of public service delivery. There are three main reasons for this result:

- The effect of civil servant behavior is rather easily quantifiable because most agents ultimately have to collect taxes and revenues, which are easily quantifiable. In contrast, the behavior of civil servants who are in charge of environmental protection or infrastructure design, for instance, is not so easily quantifiable.
- Information technology use is central to tax administrations, even in developing countries, and has been put in place in most countries

worldwide. Hence, in most developing countries, tax administrations are clearly ahead of the other public institutions.

- Changing behavior of key individuals has a macroeconomic effect. In Cameroon, changing behavior (at the margin) has led to additional revenues of several dozen million U.S. dollars (all other things being equal). Such a result would be much more difficult to obtain with a similar reform in other public institutions. Therefore, support at high levels is likely to be gained for performance measurement initiatives as soon as they yield results.

The "Gaming Effect"

Measurement is common in most customs administrations but frequently is a blunt instrument pursued for primitive accountability reasons or for reaching arbitrarily set objectives, such as revenue targets. Measurement in customs frequently has a rather limited influence and can have perverse effects (see chapter 2 for the adverse impact on Cameroon Customs).

The "gaming effect" is well known in the literature about performance measurement and contracts performance (see Bevan and Hood 2005), because there is a risk of reduced performance where targets do not apply, which is detrimental to the overall reform. It is crucial to keep in mind that, by themselves, indicators "provide an incomplete and inaccurate picture" and therefore cannot wholly capture the reality on the ground (Bevan and Hood 2005, 7).

Measurement, like any activity, is a time constraint, which creates risks. Above all, there is a risk of data manipulation (Mookherjee 2004).[4] Moreover, excessive emphasis on measurement can create opportunity costs away from the key objective of the organization, such as revenue collection or antismuggling initiatives.

Measurement indicators must be carefully chosen to ensure that knowledge is being uncovered, not hidden. As Rossi, Lipsey, and Freeman (2004, 222) state, "A measure that is poorly chosen or poorly conceived can completely undermine the worth of an impact assessment by producing misleading estimates. Only if outcome measures are valid, reliable, and appropriately sensitive can impact assessments be regarded as credible."

As Bevan and Hood (2005) point out, there is *no* game-proof design. It is merely essential to maintain focus on this obstacle and adapt continuously the performance measurement system.

The Importance of Experimenting and Evaluating

Measurement, for purposes of reform, should not be "copied and pasted" from one country to another. Due consideration must be given to the varying aims of the customs service and the specific political, social, economic, and administrative conditions in the country.

When advocating any strategy, one should use caution to ensure that it is not taken too far or overemphasized. Moreover, measurement is, of course, not the only approach to improve the collection and analysis of information. We would be disappointed if measurement became the only reform technique. Although we recommend measurement as a priority, we do not discount qualitative information gathering. Thus, we contend that measurement and experimentation can be supplemented by systematic qualitative analysis. Qualitative information can serve to fuel insights into the core problems and, if sufficiently robust, can provide a deeper understanding of reality. Comprehensive interviews with stakeholders who are willing to provide useful and accurate information can greatly supplement quantitative information.

Experiments and quasi-experiments (Campbell and Stanley 1963) should be encouraged in customs and tax reform. While randomized controlled trials (RCTs) are increasingly applied in development assistance (Banerjee and Duflo 2011), they appear to be infrequently used to study customs or tax reform. We do not believe, however, that RCTs are infeasible in this context, and their usage should increase. When it is not possible to apply RCTs, we advocate the use of quasi-experimental and nonrandomized designs.

Measurement applied to experimentation is also about how donors, experts, and national administrations work together. On the one hand, national administrations in developing countries ask for technical assistance, standards, and expertise that are based on experiences of developing countries and use experts from such countries. These requests encourage the dissemination of such models. On the other hand, reforms of customs or tax administrations are represented as semifailures in terms of the initial expected outcomes set by donors and politicians (Zake 2011). Beyond fiscal authorities, this viewpoint is part of a global representation extended to all kinds of change in developing countries. For instance, Mbembe (1989) recalls that Sub-Saharan Africa has been portrayed as an area resistant to administrative organization for ages, inimical to trade, and under constant economic threat. Reform projects conducted with donors may fuel this representation: usually the end of a reform is the time when donors and local administrations become aware of the gaps of their own representations of success. This gap between local officials and international experts has been extensively analyzed (Olivier de Sardan 1995).

This situation calls for a more accurate assessment of the real conditions in which the state operates. Reform by numbers should be part of the solution to avoid the trap of the usual and disputed representation of failure or success. First, criteria of success may be quantitative and calculated thanks to data related to the condition of the administration before the launch of the reform. This accurate preevaluation of reality is a way to design tangible criteria of success for the coming reform. Second, when they continuously measure some specific parameters (delays, revenue collection, bad practices), experts and officials jointly generate a kind of historical dimension of the administration, as a way to balance the fact that all expected initial outcomes may not have been reached at the end of the project in order to pave the way for a real evaluation of change. Indeed, experts and donors have to agree that "ownership," which is advocated by the 2008 Declaration of Paris on the Public Aid, has its counterpart: sometimes unexpected results are achieved whereas expected ones are not. Measurement is a way to define, jointly and initially, what successful ownership could be.

The Importance of Details

Performance measurement is a useful tool, but its success (or lack of success) depends on some key features, which need to be taken into account for future reform designs:

- Knowledge of internal political economy and redistribution schemes in a tax administration is critical.
- Technical assistance (with development of tools, such as mirror statistics studies, monthly performance reports, and discussions) is crucial, whereas lending and funding can have perverse effects (see Rajaram, Raballand, and Palale 2010).
- Gradual change should be sought, building on past performance and successes.

Presentation of This Book

The book's chapters track the two main measurement functions used in fiscal administrations: measuring performance and modernizing control techniques thanks to the use of measurement. This caesura may seem artificial: all measurement policies and approaches share the same overall goal of improving government effectiveness and efficiency, either by improving the control performance of the service or by developing analysis tools for mitigating fraud. Nevertheless, applying measurement to the practices of civil servants and users meets specific goals that change behavior and fight corruption. Measurement is used to improve internal control audit and the appropriate execution of administrative procedures. In this context, quantification raises resistance because it is part of a deep reform of the professional culture. Alternatively, using measurement to modernize customs techniques is not easier but raises different, more strategic issues, such as the adequacy of figures to represent reality and, therefore, the effectiveness of the new tools to complement or even replace old control techniques that were also empirical.

Although most chapters provide knowledge about the national context and the implementation policy of measurement, chapters 2–4 are more concerned with describing the political and internal motivations, the resistances, and the effects of measurement. As such, the case studies that are presented directly relate to the measurement of customs performance.

In chapter 2, Samson Bilangna and Marcellin Djeuwo from the Cameroon customs administration present the history and the outcomes of the performance measurement policy launched by their administration: the General Directorate of Customs signed "performance contracts" with the frontline customs officers in 2010 and with some importers in 2011. Performance measurement is not new to the revenue agencies in Cameroon, but its association with individual contracts has dramatically changed the hierarchical relationships and the relationships to users. Bilangna and Djeuwo's work is fueled by two years of monthly monitoring, which is a good example of the dual function of quantification: measuring individual and team performances and also measuring the effects of this transparent measurement of performance. Indeed, in many cases, administrative reforms fall into the trap of a representation of failure, which is deeply rooted in experts' minds and often legitimated by poor or deceptive quantifiable results: results of public service reforms are considered either incomplete or different from the original objectives, but these evaluations are often qualitative judgments. By monitoring a few quantitative parameters (such as clearance delays, fraud, customs revenues) before and after the launch of the measurement policy, Bilangna and Djeuwo demonstrate the positive effects of combining quantification and contracting in the context of a policy launched to fight against bad practices, especially corruption and weak technical knowledge.

In chapter 3, José-María Muñoz, an anthropologist, offers a complementary view of the introduction of figures in the Cameroon tax administration. His analysis focuses less on the production of numbers and more on their social use: how the revenue targets that are assigned to the tax administration—through DPO (that is, *direction par objectifs*, or management by objectives)—and that are developed at the national level drive locally the administrative action in a region of Cameroon. His analysis also focuses on what extent this policy generates new practices of accountability and transparency among the tax authority, the political authority, and the public. Muñoz highlights the arrangement between new practices emerging and the appearance and circulation of new words associated with them. This arrangement contributes to a demonstration of technical power by the state to citizens and donors. One of the chapter's insights shows the genesis of this policy and the dynamic concept of measurement that is circulating between developed and developing countries. If the theory of NPM and its application by the French government probably influenced the design and adoption of DPO in Cameroon, the fact remains that the Cameroonian government has also transformed and adapted concepts to its own environment. Finally, Muñoz also shows that if all Cameroonian authorities were instructed to adopt a form of DPO, the customs and tax administrations would develop their own policies faster and with more efficiency than any other administration, a fact that reinforces the idea of a specific relation between tax authorities and numbers.

The fourth chapter ends the book's first part, which focuses on performance measurement. Xavier Pascual from the French customs administration describes the system implemented by his administration to measure the collective performance of customs units and bureaus. This French example illustrates the diversity of possible approaches and makes more apparent the specific issues that developing countries seek to solve using performance measurement. For instance, unlike customs administration in Cameroon, the French customs administration has not developed individual measurement. French tools for measuring performance respond to political demands and budget constraints, which require the administration to account more accurately for the funds allocated by the political level and to fully exercise its management autonomy to better distribute its resources in the territory. However, from this case study, one can also draw parallels between the approaches used by developed and developing countries. First, establishing performance measurement is a slow and sometimes very adaptable process because of the need to adjust to new conditions or information. Although numbers are always associated with objectivity and robustness, Pascual provides a multiscalar analysis, recalling the multiple steps to install a sustainable performance measurement policy. As a second parallel between developed and developing countries, figures support objectivity and pacify hierarchical relations: in France, deciding on the implementation, the removal, or the relocation of customs units has major effects on the daily life of civil servants and can generate internal tensions. Such tensions can also arise in Cameroon, where rewarding those inspectors who have good practices and punishing those who have bad ones has a major social influence. Because of their ability to foster common understanding, numbers can ground serene discussions between actors when some of them have power and authority over the others, either within an administrative hierarchy or within relationships between users and officers.

The second line of research in the field of measurement specifically concerns techniques that use measurement as a way to improve the traditional customs function, which is to control commodity flows and facilitate legal trade. The innovation described in the four following chapters is making extensive use of data stored by automated customs clearance systems. All customs administrations have their own automated system to lodge and clear declarations; accordingly, customs administrations store substantial data related to time, goods, and stakeholders. Unfortunately, social scientists and public administrators exploit these databases inadequately. The case studies in chapters 5–8 demonstrate the potential uses of data to improve traditional customs functions.

In chapter 5, Anne-Marie Geourjon and Bertrand Laporte, who are both economists, and Ousmane Coundoul and Massène Gadiaga, who are from the Senegalese customs administration, present the use of data mining to select imports for inspection. This project is being developed in Senegal and embodies the concept of risk analysis. Although this approach is widespread in the customs community, few concrete applications have been presented and analyzed in the literature. In developing countries, risk analysis is often limited to the injunction to control less, thanks to empirical analysis. Customs officials are encouraged to conduct controls after customs clearance; in developing countries, however, administrations face many challenges that undermine the reliability and feasibility of such controls. An innovation of the authors is to use automated data mining and scoring techniques to guide declarations into various control circuits.

A second innovation is the use of measurement to estimate the effectiveness of the technique. Geourjon, Laporte, Coundoul, and Gadiaga have applied their system to a body of existing data, and the results are convincing: the system is still able to find 80 percent of fraud cases when it applies a control rate divided by 2.6. Finally, the authors emphasize measurement tools as a way to improve the working environment and culture, because, for instance, the automation of declarations selectivity may be a way to fight against corruption and poor technical skills.

Sharing the same global aim to make controls more efficient, economists Gaël Raballand and Guillermo Arenas from the World Bank and anthropologist Thomas Cantens from the World Customs Organization suggest, in chapter 6, using mirror statistics to detect potentially fraudulent import flows. Mirror statistics calculate the gaps of foreign trade statistics between two trading partner countries. Comparing imports extracted from the Cameroonian customs clearance system and exports of the partner countries to Cameroon, extracted from the public database UN Comtrade (United Nations Commodity Trade Statistics Database), Raballand and Cantens show that it is possible to detect and measure different types of fraud on imports in Cameroon: undervaluation, Harmonized System misclassifications to lower the fiscal pressure, overvaluation, fraud on quantities, and so forth. This kind of analysis also assesses the positive and negative effects of fraud on customs revenue. Mirror statistics are often criticized by economists who consider the unreliability of customs data as a major obstacle to their use. Paradoxically, it is this lack of "reliability" of numbers that is both the problem and the solution. When used pragmatically to orient customs controls in the field, mirror statistics do not seek to account for the accuracy of the flow of goods but the existence of inaccuracies in statements on these flows. In addition, as part of the agreement of the World Trade Organization on customs valuation, these statistics can provide evidence to customs to challenge the values declared on fake invoices that are presented at the border.

Hanane Benyagoub, Hakim Nait Abdelselam, and Aissa Boudergui from Algerian customs are also interested in customs fraud. Chapter 7 relates to smuggling and the sociopolitical issues that measurement may unveil. Benyagoub, Abdelselam, and Boudergui describe a system that monitors fraud cases from their detection to their legal conclusion. This system both reports on performance and tracks the progress of prosecutions. It improves the efficiency of the customs service in charge of treating fraud cases after their detection. This approach responds to two needs that the Algerian customs officers quickly identified when they invested in an antismuggling policy. Algerian customs had deployed substantial material and legal resources against smuggling, but this new administrative arrangement was to be accompanied by an informed debate on its effectiveness. The global performance measurement system implemented a few years earlier, however, did not make possible the automated collection of performance data related to fraud. Automated collection is often simple for clearance time, nature of goods, and stakeholders because all customs declarations are processed by the information technology customs clearance system. Obviously, this is not the case for smuggling, and data related to smuggling were to be lodged manually in the performance measurement system, which raised many issues of reliability and opportunity. The system presented by Benyagoub, Abdelselam, and Boudergui has been set up to overcome these two problems that are common to all customs administrations. It measures both the evolution of a phenomenon of smuggling, which is, by nature, very flexible, and the adaptation of the customs units on the ground. It also organizes the automatic circulation of this information within the service to favor spatial distribution of resources and to compare unit efficiency. Finally, the authors point out the need to use data, by profiling fraudsters, to inform public debate on the law and the way society deals with smugglers.

To conclude the second part on the integration of measurement in information systems, Soyoung Yang from the Korea Customs Service (KCS), in chapter 8, offers a case study on KCS's implementation of a single window system. With respect to risk analysis, the concept of single window is widespread in the trade and customs environments, but few concrete achievements have been presented and analyzed. The novelty of this chapter is that it places the measurement in the heart of two perspectives: that of the economic operators and that of the administration that is at their service. First, quantitative analysis can demonstrate the effectiveness of the new system that reduced clearance times. Second, quantitative analysis can also show that the savings made through trade facilitation exceed public investment, which is an effective exercise of transparency of public expenditure.

Notes

1. The translation is from the English version of the book (Benveniste 1973).
2. In trade and customs development papers, the terms *development assistance, reform, modernization,* and *capacity building* are generally used interchangeably. A subtle nuance that appears occasionally is that development assistance

generally has a donor-provided slant, whereas capacity building can imply beneficiary-driven effectiveness and efficiency improvements. Reform and modernization can encompass donor- or beneficiary-driven improvement efforts or a blending of both.

3. Customs also has other responsibilities, particularly countering smuggling in illicit goods such as narcotics, counterfeit goods, and endangered species. Moreover, taxation seems to play a role in state building and accountability (Moore 2007).

4. This possibility is also why independent audits of performance are important and why surveys and qualitative information can also help to identify manipulations.

References

Banerjee, Abhijit, and Esther Duflo. 2011. *Poor Economics: A Radical Rethinking of the Way to Fight Global Poverty*. New York: PublicAffairs.

Behn, Robert D. 2003. "Why Measure Performance? Different Purposes Require Different Measures." *Public Administration Review* 63 (5): 586–606.

Benveniste, Émile. 1969. *Le vocabulaire des institutions indo-européennes*. Vols. 1 and 2. Paris: Les Editions de Minuit.

———. 1973. *Indo-European Language and Society*. Translated by Elizabeth Palmer. London: Faber & Faber.

Bevan, Gwyn, and Christopher Hood. 2005. "What's Measured Is What Matters: Targets and Gaming in the English Public Health Care System. PSP Discussion Paper 0501, Public Services Programme, Economic and Social Research Council, Swindon, U.K. http://www.publicservices.ac.uk/wp-content/uploads/dp0501.pdf.

Bigsten, Arne, Jan Willem Gunning, and Finn Tarp. 2006. "The Effectiveness of Foreign Aid: Overview and an Evaluation Proposal." Swedish International Development Cooperation Agency, Stockholm.

Campbell, Donald T., and Julian C. Stanley. 1963. *Experimental and Quasi-Experimental Designs for Research*. Boston: Houghton Mifflin.

IDS (Institute of Development Studies). 2010. *An Upside-Down View of Governance*. London: University of Sussex.

Mbembe, Achille. 1989. "Pouvoir, violence et accumulation." *Politique Africaine* 39: 7–24.

Mookherjee, Dilip. 2004. *The Crisis in Government Accountability: Essays on Governance Reforms and India's Economic Performance*. New York: Oxford University Press.

Moore, Mick. 2007. "How Does Taxation Affect the Quality of Governance?" IDS Working Paper 280, Institute of Development Studies, University of Sussex, Brighton, U.K.

Olivier de Sardan, Jean-Pierre. 1995. *Anthropologie et développement: Essai en socio-anthropologie du changement social.* Paris: Éditions Karthala.

Rajaram, Anand, Gaël Raballand, and Patricia Palale. 2010. "Public Sector Reform: Changing Behavior with Cars and Computers?" *Africa Can … End Poverty* (blog), February 16. http://blogs.worldbank.org/africacan/public-sector-reform-changing-behavior-with-cars-and-computers.

Rossi, Peter H., Mark W. Lipsey, and Howard E. Freeman. 2004. *Evaluation: A Systematic Approach.* 7th ed. Thousand Oaks, CA: Sage.

Zake, Justin. 2011. "Customs Administration Reform and Modernization in Anglophone Africa: Early 1990s to Mid-2010." IMF Working Paper 11/184, International Monetary Fund, Washington, DC.

CHAPTER 2

The Figures Culture in Cameroon Customs

From Allocations of Budget Estimates to Performance Measurement

Samson Bilangna and Marcellin Djeuwo

The aim of this chapter is to illustrate how the handling of "numbers" in Cameroon Customs assessments has moved from a straightforward arithmetical calculation (dividing budgetary estimates by the number of customs units) to a more pragmatic approach based on a true assessment of individual and collective performances in service delivery, but still using numbers as its foundation. It involves seeing how quantification can be used to produce different outcomes, depending on the tools used and approach taken, and showing how the same numbers can be used differently and thus produce different results.

The role of a customs administration is broadly to provide three essential services: collection of customs revenues; protection of the economic area and the general public; and, because of its presence at border posts, assistance to other public authorities. Of those three services, the collection of customs revenues always takes precedence in developing countries to such an extent that attainment of budget objectives becomes the sole true indicator of head customs officers' performance and that of their chains of command. How could the situation be any different, given that some customs administrations have responsibility for over 50 percent of public resources, the very resources that allow the government to address the many responsibilities it faces? Customs revenues have a special importance here, and undercollection or noncollection can play a role in destabilizing the state itself. Insofar as Cameroon is concerned specifically, customs revenues have often accounted for more than 20 percent of the state budget (Libom Li Likeng, Cantens, and Bilangna 2009), further increasing the importance of their collection. To explain this issue more fully, we will demonstrate the importance of figures in customs revenues collection, then move on to outline the perverse effects of this approach, and finally describe briefly the current approach and the initial results it has produced.

Use of Numbers in Cameroon Customs: The Management by Objectives Method in the 1990s

"Results culture" is a model that is recognized in the management methods espoused by U.S. companies and is explained in detail in English-language management literature. It led to an upsurge over several years in "objective-based contracts" and "results-based bonuses" in the United States, then in France, in the 1980s.

The concept was introduced into Cameroon, at the Ministry of Finance, under the fiscal and customs reforms of 1994. The new era heralded a different approach to management in the fiscal and customs administrations: management by objectives (MBO)[1] was subsequently adopted as the operational strategy by which to spread the results-based culture within the Directorate General of Customs and the Directorate General of Taxation. The word *performance*, rarely used in official statements, gradually began to be of interest to senior officials in the Ministry of Finance.

The structural adjustment plans intended to support African economies dependent on subsidies presented an opportunity for donor agencies to take a close interest in the running of taxation authorities in Africa, particularly customs administrations. The donor agencies pressed for reform in the Cameroon customs administration, in particular in relation to the collection of customs revenues. As a demonstration of its good faith and efforts made, and to placate the ever-increasing demands of public opinion, Cameroon Customs regularly published the amount of duties it collected in its journal, *Revue des douanes camerounaises* (*Cameroon Customs Review*). Consequently, the amount of revenue collected became an important number to the community as a whole. Even the donor agencies, in conducting their reviews, were essentially evaluating the raising of customs revenues in the light of figures representing actual outcomes and exemptions granted. Exemptions, in particular, were the subject of close scrutiny by donor agencies—to the point where expertise in that area became one of the principal performance evaluation criteria in the public finance sector in Cameroon.

Between 1999 and 2003, the customs aspect of that procedure was enhanced by the Customs Administration Reform and Rehabilitation Plan, which proposed 71 measures structured around 193 actions, all aimed at modernizing Cameroon Customs. The new framework also required profound change in management methods within the ministry and a full understanding by the principal managers of the concept of *management* as "a human and social activity seeking to encourage particular behaviors, motivate teams and groups, develop organizational structures, and conduct the activities of an organization with a view to achieving a given level of performance" (Plane 2003, 3).

At the beginning of each fiscal year, Cameroon's parliament sets a quantified target for the customs administration. All activities performed by customs (fighting against fraud and counterfeiting, facilitating trade, adopting good practices, combating corruption, and so on) are evaluated only in the light of the revenues collected. That background gave rise to MBO. At that time, the minister for finance, who was ultimately responsible for fiscal and customs revenues, would allocate state budget contributions to the various administrations as provided for in the Finance Law. Each director general was required to allocate the budget to the various chains of command within his or her administration so that the heads of the chains of command could do the same for their various component bodies. Each customs entity was therefore quantifiable and could be expressed as an amount of money to be collected. The evaluation meeting's agenda then required each manager to answer two arithmetical questions: how much have you collected and how much do you still have to collect? All monthly or quarterly assessment meetings revolved around the figures, and each manager was assessed solely on the basis of his quantified results.

The head of the Coastal Region customs office (the regional director), who is responsible for collection of almost 80 percent of customs revenues, devised two quantity-based strategies to obtain his staff's total commitment to attaining the expected results: the hit parade technique and the daily tally of results.

The first strategy, in which his aim was to encourage his colleagues to emulate each other, was to publish the total amount of customs duties adjusted and fines imposed by each officer for the month. His staff members were ranked according to their contribution to the actual revenue raised in their chain of command. The staff always dreaded the monthly publication of the result, but it was much heralded by the press. There were always (negative) explanations for the (under)performance of customs inspector X or Y, who became a source of derision. To avoid negative coverage in the press and public opinion, the customs officers made an effort to monitor their own performance to satisfy their superiors' expectations.

In the second strategy, the department head kept a file tracking the amount of taxes expected for that month, the amount actually raised daily to the current date, the amount outstanding, and the number of days left in the month in which the outstanding amount could be raised. This file allowed daily monitoring of progress toward the revenue target. Each head of a chain of command could assess the ground yet to be covered and the means he or she could deploy to that end. The files dictated the atmosphere in offices: when the files were good because the level of revenue was acceptable, senior staff members were welcoming and could be approached easily; if the opposite was the case, they pressured everyone, and the smallest slip in behavior could result in punishment. Although this strategy was a nod to a concept developed by Drucker ([1954] 2007), mistakes were made in the way the concept was applied. According to Drucker, MBO was essentially a participatory approach to target setting. Drucker was of the view that a significant aspect of MBO was to measure and compare actual employee performance with the established norms, the idea being that employees are more inclined to discharge their responsibilities when they have been involved in setting their targets and choosing the actions they are to take.

In fact, the numbers submitted did not always give management a good feel for the actual situation on the ground because the asymmetry of information sometimes gave officers (with operational responsibilities) a monopoly of power over the director general of customs (Cartier-Bresson 2008). The result was the frequent misuse of an approach to assessment that did, in fact, have some advantages.

The Perverse Effects or Misuse of a Method of Performance Evaluation

Cameroon Customs was aware of the weakness of the means available to fight against customs fraud and corruption and so negotiated with economic operators on a sector-by-sector basis to establish a minimum sum payable on import. Cameroon shares a border more than 1,000 kilometers long with its powerful neighbor, Nigeria, and has an extensive maritime shore. The lack of materiel, the weakness of the customs staff, the ingenuity of fraudsters, and the dubious ethical standards of some officers mean that the land and maritime borders are very porous. Importers therefore have considerable freedom to choose whether to go through customs or to import illegally; the only risk inherent in illegal importing is a chance encounter with customs officers, who are open to "negotiations," whether official or unofficial, on the customs duties. To forestall such scenarios, the customs administration much preferred to work with importers, sometimes only just within the law, to establish mutually agreed amounts payable, based on the type of import or the type of packaging. Customs was unquestionably seeking merely to implement the principle that any out-of-court arrangement, however bad, is better than successful legal proceedings. Here, too, the figures transformed a bad arrangement into a good means of attaining the expected results. In short, the numbers establish the threshold of acceptability for bad practices. The revenues target itself is merely a threshold of acceptability for corruption (Cantens 2009).

Some customs officers took advantage of the situation to devise a number of bad practices. In one case, some officers in outlying areas where procedures are conducted manually collected revenue up front but transferred to the state coffers only enough to satisfy the target set by the chain of command, retaining a "safety cushion" to make up any shortfall that might occur in future months. The customs officer would carry a portion of revenues from month m over to the following month to give the superior hierarchy the impression that the officer was working hard.

In the airport's computerized offices, the practice has always been to use a simplified system known as the air waybill slip (AWB/S) to clear goods for release without a customs declaration. This practice involves releasing goods following signature of the AWB/S and granting the user (or the user's representative) a deadline by which to conclude the declaration formalities. In reality, the purpose of this procedure, which amounts to an exemption, is to facilitate the rapid release of certain perishable goods that could deteriorate or devalue if held in warehouses awaiting customs clearance (daily newspapers, flowering plants, mortal remains, vaccines that have to be kept at a particular temperature, and the like). Hence, the head of the office retains the right to vary the clearance of accounts depending on how the figure for the month's revenues develops over time. When that figure is healthy in relation to the monthly targets, very little adjustment occurs; in the contrary situation, adjustments may be frequent. The risk inherent in this practice is that, in an automated system, an important part of the work is done manually, with the obvious risks of loss that this omission implies. At the principal customs office at Douala International Airport, the number of AWB/Ss requiring adjustment sometimes amounts to half the month's transactions, and some AWB/Ss dated several years ago have not yet been finalized.

The other major bad practice was to produce fanciful assessments of duties in full knowledge that the user was being burdened with an unrecoverable debt that was wholly unjustifiable. The aim of the game here was for an officer to artificially fulfill the requirements of his or her contract with the hierarchy. The practice was sometimes also engaged in at a strategic level.

Often these assessments meant that the best figures in an entire year were achieved in the final month, with some of these same assessments then being canceled at the beginning of the following fiscal year after being used to give the impression that the quantified targets for the year they related to had been attained. To correct that failing, the customs hierarchy introduced a requirement for performance assessment to follow the cash-basis principle; from that point onward, the principal measure of performance would have to be the amount actually recovered.

Another frequent practice was the erroneous allocation of revenue. The customs administration levies budgetary revenues, which are intended to be fed into the state budget, and extrabudgetary revenues, which are automatically earmarked for specific purposes or particular public institutions. A distinction is drawn between these two types of customs revenues during the assessment process. The tendency observed on the ground in customs offices where processes are still manual is for all revenues to be systematically allocated to the state budget to meet the MBO, thereby penalizing other bodies whose operation depends exclusively on these resources. Some officers in *non*computerized customs offices assessed and collected computer fees, which ought to be levied only in computerized customs units. Finally, the allocation of budget estimates led to gimmicks in border customs offices, where local customs chiefs indulged in marketing to attract service users to their offices with the aim of reaching their revenue targets. This practice would not be unhealthy if it sought to bring in users who habitually evaded customs offices. However, it became unhealthy when users were dissuaded from going to customs office A on the promise that customs office B would offer more favorable customs clearance terms. Consequently, the target attained by that means at customs office B would be counterbalanced by the ensuing larger drop in revenue at customs office A, and progress toward the attainment of customs targets as a whole would fall short of the mark. Indeed, such a practice amounts to a traffic diversion under an objective explanation: the MBO.

A major constraint of the MBO system was that its sole target was the amount collected in duties and taxes, with no requirement to establish how and why that target was attained. The quality of service rendered; the interests of economic operators; the identification of clear, precise indicators drawn up on objective, quantifiable bases; and the definition of performance assessment criteria are other factors that must be taken into account. The next section outlines the various stages in the current process.

From the Production of Indicators to Contracting: Procedures Constructed around Numbers

The business world's pressing demand for facilitation and the need to comply with international conventions on good practices forced Cameroon Customs to alter its method of choice without abandoning its revered numbers. Since then, numbers have been used to reconcile revenue collection, to facilitate trade, and to fight dishonest conduct.

As part of the implementation of its reform program, Cameroon Customs adopted the ASYCUDA++[2] computerized system in 2007. The system was introduced into a hostile environment in which strong resistance to change, pessimistic talk about the genuine success of the system, and attacks in the press against the customs hierarchy were the rule. It became clear that Cameroon Customs needed to provide the press and public opinion with an explanation of the objective, quantifiable data produced by the ASYCUDA database. The figures came to the rescue, confounding the system's detractors and anticipating potential bottlenecks those detractors might have created. It churned out figures daily, reporting not only the customs revenue figures but also the actual activity of officers on the new computer system. The opportunities that

ASYCUDA provides for monitoring activity meant that, for example, the length of time that specific officers were connected could be reported, as could the actions recorded on the system. Weekly statements were sent to the minister not only by way of a report to the government but also to inform public opinion, which was concerned about the loss of customs revenues reported in the press (Cantens 2007).

ASYCUDA data were used to launch a performance indicators policy to ensure that sustainable support would be provided to modernize Cameroon Customs. Since January 2008, 24 (later 31) indicators have been produced every month for 11 offices in Douala. The indicators track customs activity to place in context the variations in results achieved by each office. The level of detail used means that the performance of individual officers and members of partner professions can be measured.[3] The indicators also monitor sensitive customs procedures to provide managers with information on the activity being carried out by their department and its officers. Finally, indicators serve to fight fraud by ensuring compliance with control guidelines provided under risk management procedures. Customs has thus strengthened the internal operational control system, which has helped correct information asymmetry between central services and operational services (Libom Li Likeng, Cantens, and Bilangna 2009). The system, christened "gazing into the mirror," produced a form of self-regulation, thereby triggering a reduction in a number of bad practices and corruption.

However, these indicators merely presented a snapshot that describes operations in customs or provides a fair account of them. To move beyond this purely descriptive system of indicators and toward a prescriptive approach, Cameroon Customs developed performance contracts. These contracts are genuinely bilateral agreements signed by the director general of customs and the frontline inspectors who are responsible for 76 percent of the revenue collected at the port of Douala, the principal point of entry for goods into Cameroonian territory. Broadly speaking, 92 percent of all customs revenues are collected at the Douala port and airport.

In a bid to reconcile trade facilitation with effective efforts to fight both fraud and bad practices, eight indicators were defined (four for each category). The indicators were drawn up using the objective, quantifiable data produced directly by ASYCUDA and are the benchmarks for assessing the performance of inspectors and individuals with operational responsibilities.

For all practical purposes, the list of indicators can be revised to take account of discussions or the relevance of various indicators in light of changes in the situation that led to their introduction. Against that background, pursuant to contract provisions, some indicators were amended following the second six-month evaluation, and contracts currently contain 10 indicators. Monitoring of operations and customs clearance processes is better as a result.

Some of the Results from the New Method

The new way in which figures are being used has led to many positive results.

Inspectors' Contracts

The effect of the contracts with inspectors is fairly substantial in terms of improvement in processing times, which was a direct result of the decline in the bad practices that overshadowed the relationship between importers and inspectors.

The first bad practice was to assess a declaration and then enter it at a later time. This procedure is contrary to accepted customs practice and can be used by an inspector to his personal advantage. This practice has declined noticeably. The number of declarations assessed in the yellow channel then amended subsequently by the same inspector fell by 49 percent between the period before the contracts came into effect (2009) and 2011 (table 2.1).[4]

The second bad practice stemmed from the power conferred on inspectors to reroute declarations from a facilitation channel to a control channel that placed greater constraints on importers.[5] An inspector was able to use rerouting to exert pressure on importers. The contracts established a framework for this power by requiring that inspectors significantly increase the proportion of declarations involving disputed claims that they routed away from the facilitation channel and to the channel

Table 2.1   Delayed Entry of Customs Assessments

Customs office	Number of entries			Decrease from 2009 to 2011	
	2009	2010	2011	Number	Percent
Douala International Airport	2,605	2,469	2,162	−443	−17
Douala Port I	2,854	2,357	487	−2,367	−83
Douala Port V	1,876	1,519	751	−1,125	−60
Douala external warehouse	875	781	787	−88	−10
Total	8,210	7,126	4,187	−4,023	−49

Source: Cameroon Customs information system.

that required scanners and physical inspection of goods, with the understanding that the inspector's decision had to be based on a stronger suspicion of fraud than that produced by ASYCUDA.

The contracts have had a significant effect: the number of adjusted declarations as a proportion of all declarations rerouted from the yellow to the red channel was 60 percent at Douala Port I and 92 percent at Douala Port V during the third quarter of 2011. The rates for the same period in 2010 were 29 percent and 55 percent, respectively. The rate averaged only 8 percent in 2009 (that is, before the contracts) in both offices (table 2.2).

The third bad practice was competition between frontline inspectors. The number of declarations on file is important: the more declarations an inspector processes, the greater the number of frauds he or she can find and the greater the inspector's opportunities to earn money, whether by honest or dishonest means. By misusing the computer system, some inspectors were able to process up to five times more declarations than their colleagues. Competition of this kind was dangerous because some inspectors tried to be "more understanding" than others with importers. Fortunately, the disparity in workload between the inspector processing the highest number of declarations and the one processing the lowest number is closing. The current trend shows that the busiest inspector has about twice as many declarations as the least busy inspector in the office.

The fourth bad practice was when an inspector arrived at work late and stayed in the office for only a very brief time. Now time at work starts when an inspector records the first operation of the day in the ASYCUDA system and ends with the entry by the same inspector of the day's final operation. By that criterion, time at work has risen in comparison with the third quarter of 2010 in almost all offices. This improvement is most visible at Douala Port V, where time at work increased from 5 hours and 56 minutes in 2009 to 6 hours and 32 minutes in 2010 and then to 7 hours and 30 minutes in 2011 (table 2.3).

Table 2.2   Percentage of Adjusted Declarations as a Proportion of All Declarations Rerouted from the Yellow to the Red Channel

Customs office	Adjusted declarations (%)					Change from 2009 to 2011 (%)
	2008	2009	2010	2011	2012	
Douala Port I	0	7	29	60	75	+53
Douala Port V	15	9	55	92	91	+83
Average	7.5	8	42	76	83	+68

Source: Cameroon Customs information system.

Table 2.3   Customs Inspectors' Hours at Work

Customs office	Time at work				2010–11 range (%)	2009–11 range (%)
	2009	2010	2011	2012		
Douala International Airport	4 hours, 39 minutes	4 hours, 38 minutes	5 hours, 5 minutes	5 hours, 10 minutes	9.50	9.3
Douala Port I	6 hours, 17 minutes	6 hours, 25 minutes	7 hours	7 hours, 11 minutes	9.16	11.4
Douala Port V	5 hours, 56 minutes	6 hours, 32 minutes	7 hours, 30 minutes	7 hours, 36 minutes	14.68	26.3

Source: Cameroon Customs information system.

The positive effects of the decline in bad practices on the provision of services covered by a performance contract (Douala Ports I and V since February 2010; Douala external warehouses and Douala International Airport since January 2011)[6] can be evaluated using two qualitative indicators: time spent processing files and efforts to fight fraud.

The data extracted from ASYCUDA make clear that the time between registration of a declaration by a broker and assessment by an inspector is falling all the time. In Douala Port V, it is now 24 minutes, compared with 2 hours and 37 minutes for the same period in 2010. In Douala Port I, it is now 1 hour and 14 minutes as against 4 hours and 22 minutes last year. Before the introduction of contracts in 2009, the average time between registration of a declaration by a broker and assessment by an inspector was 16 hours.

The Douala external warehouse office (to take just one example) was brought under contract in 2011. The time spent by that office on processing a file fell from 32 hours in 2010 to 9 hours in 2011. The file-processing time was around 68 hours in 2009. During the same period, the fall in the time taken to process files did not follow the same curve in the neighboring office that was not under contract. There, the time fell from 44 hours and 33 minutes in August–October 2009, to 37 hours and 16 minutes, and then to 16 hours and 51 minutes for the same period in 2010 and 2011, respectively.

Clearly, the extensive time spent processing files can be used to exert pressure on importers, especially in an environment where time, more than anything else, is money. The number of declarations processed on the day of registration is rising in offices under contract. At Douala Port I, 90 percent of files were processed on the day of registration in 2009; that percentage rose to 97.1 percent and then to 99.1 percent in 2010 and

2011, respectively. At Douala Port V, the rate rose from 93.1 percent in 2009 to 98.4 percent and then to 99.8 percent in 2010 and 2011, respectively. In the offices not under contract, the average rate rose from 78 percent to 88 percent between 2009 and 2011.

Where efforts to fight fraud are under consideration, the following points are noteworthy:

- Although the overall amount of adjusted duties and taxes is falling in some offices (Douala Port I and Douala International Airport), the quality of disputed claims has improved in all offices except the airport. Inspectors have abandoned minor disputed claims, which generated harassment, in favor of more significant cases. In absolute terms, therefore, although one could argue that performance has declined, that argument collapses when placed in the context of the advantages gained by cutting the red tape that so often gives rise to corruption. Viewed in that light, a potential loss is offset by increased facilitation.
- The offices at Douala Ports I and V and Douala International Airport have achieved and exceeded their cash-basis budgetary targets by more than CFAF 8 billion.[7]

At the same time, the measures taken under inspectors' contracts, which have led to a massive fall in clearance times for goods, have had no harmful consequences to the collection of customs duties and taxes. Customs revenues have continually risen in real terms, and Cameroon Customs has achieved and exceeded all its overall targets since 2008 despite an economic environment overshadowed by financial and economic crisis. When the target was CFAF 425 billion in 2008, Cameroon Customs collected CFAF 443 billion. The rising trend in forecasts continued in 2009, and Cameroon Customs produced and exceeded expected revenues. In 2010, Cameroon Customs produced CFAF 503.8 billion compared with a target of CFAF 499 billion. In 2011, CFAF 547.5 billion was achieved as against a forecast of CFAF 550 billion, excluding the approximately CFAF 50 billion still in the process of collection. That success meant businesses could be offered enhanced facilitation and greater fairness in controls.

Operators' Contracts

The beneficial effects of performance contracts with inspectors convinced the director general of Cameroon Customs to extend contracts to certain economic operators as part of the Customs-Business Forum

(Libom Li Likeng, Djeuwo, and Bilangna 2011). Three strands form the policy of dialogue with the private sector: sharing a single environment based on objective and quantified data; determining the set of measures to take, where those measures raise more revenue without hindering facilitation; and monitoring, by all parties involved, the effective implementation of these measures on the ground, both on the customs and the noncustoms side.

The voice of the business world is being heard more clearly in the framework of the Customs-Business Forum, which has been revitalized by the performance contracts signed since January 3, 2011, with 11 importing companies. Six months later, this number had risen to 20, thereby extending a recipe that would provide inner satisfaction to engaged, motivated partners.

Performance contracts with importers are similar in concept to those of authorized economic operators, as used by many customs administrations and the World Customs Organization: the contracts provide for the grant of procedural facilities to a number of importers who meet the conditions laid down by the administration.

However, retaining the concept of performance contracts may be preferable on the following grounds:

- Contracts allow greater flexibility by regularly tailoring the facilities granted to importers for which performance is objectively and regularly measured using data produced by ASYCUDA.
- The term *performance contract* has been part of the professional culture of Cameroon Customs since February 2010. It followed from the performance indicators introduced in January 2008. Semantic continuity is advisable because it illustrates the rationale underlying the extension of the concept to other stakeholders that have dealings with customs.

In any event, under Cameroon Customs procedures, operators' contracts provide methodical preparation for establishment of authorized economic operators, according to the relevant World Customs Organization texts and using the means appropriate to Cameroonian circumstances. The features of the operators' contracts are largely the same as those of the inspectors' contracts. The targets set for importers often refer to action in advance, promptness, and proactivity. For example, a declaration should be made prior to a vessel's arrival or a payment should be made shortly after assessment. What customs is seeking to achieve by these contracts is to accelerate port operations in the general framework of increasing the competitiveness of the Douala Port and to collect its revenue more quickly. In this opening phase, six indicators were set, and evaluation showed that the effects of the facilitation channel were apparent in time scales and revenues generally.

Under the operators' contracts, Cameroon Customs grants extensive facilities to some contracting importers. The importers were selected on the basis of the volume of their activities, their solvency, and their presumed probity. For the importers, the contract means releasing around 40 percent of their goods from the Douala Port through the blue channel, in other words without customs controls, subject to a commitment to comply with specific defined indicators adopted by agreement between the parties. The blue channel percentage can be increased, depending on importer's performance. Currently, for some importers whose performance has met the requirements of their contracts, 80 percent of their goods are processed through the Douala Port without any immediate controls.

The effect of operator contracts is just as visible in the time scales involved.[8] Since January 2011, the time spent by the 11 contracted operators on processing clearance procedures has been reduced overall. Between the third quarter of 2010 and the third quarter of 2011, the processing times fell from 14.4 days to 13.6 days. Meanwhile, processing times for operators not under contract have remained very high at around 17.4 days, compared to 18.4 days for the same period in the previous year (figure 2.1). The two best operators under contract have a processing time of 10.3 days, compared to 12.7 days in 2010. The processing times of newly contracted companies have remained stable but are still very high (18.2 days as against 20.3 days).

Goods processed through the control channels (red and yellow) take on average 17.6 days to exit the port, whereas those processed through the blue channel (the channel where rapid customs clearance is guaranteed for operators with a contract) take only 13.9 days. As a reminder, the average time release at Douala Port is around 20.0 days.

In 2011, the 11 operators who entered into contracts spent less time in the various customs clearance procedures than the newly contracted operators (apart from the phase between making the payment and receiving the exit note). By way of illustration, the time that elapses between registration of the manifest and registration of the declaration, reputedly the most time-consuming stage, is around 6.0 days for the 11 original operators, compared with 11.6 days for the new operators. On the one hand, this disparity may be evidence that the original operators

Figure 2.1 Evolution of Time Scales by Operators, 2008–12

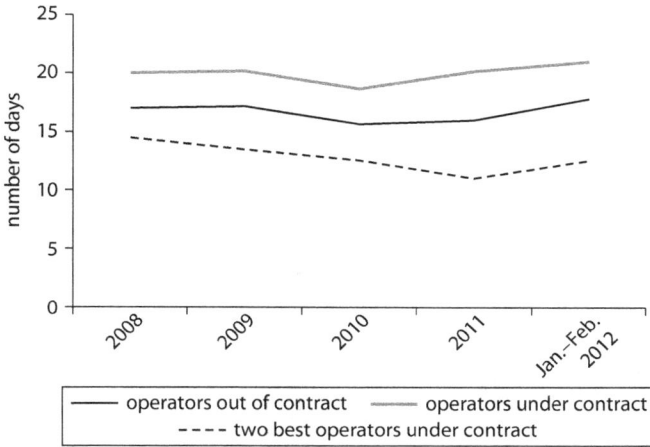

Source: Cameroon Customs information system.

act in advance of their operations more often than new operators, who for the most part are still feeling their way. On the other hand, it may indicate that the best operators, who were interested in reform and were therefore prepared or ready to improve, were selected first. The current evaluation is not yet at a point where a firm conclusion can be reached on this matter.

By granting facilities, the customs administration risked potential loss of customs revenues. The question is whether that risk was measured and contained. The answer is that it was. In fact, the duties and taxes paid and the value of imports by contracted operators have moved in the same direction (see figure 2.2).

Generally, no particular negative developments have occurred. The level of fraud has been curbed markedly, except for one operator, who alone accounts for 98 percent of amounts adjusted among contracted operators.

Conclusion

Cameroon Customs has a long-standing culture of using figures as the unit of measurement for the performance of its staff and departments. Figures have also been used as stopgaps to attain quantified targets set for departments. In some circumstances, they have been used as a shield and a safeguard. In short, anxiety over numbers has changed historically over time and space, but figures have retained their revered status.

Figure 2.2   Evolution of the Volume of Imports and the Amount of Duties Paid, 2007–12

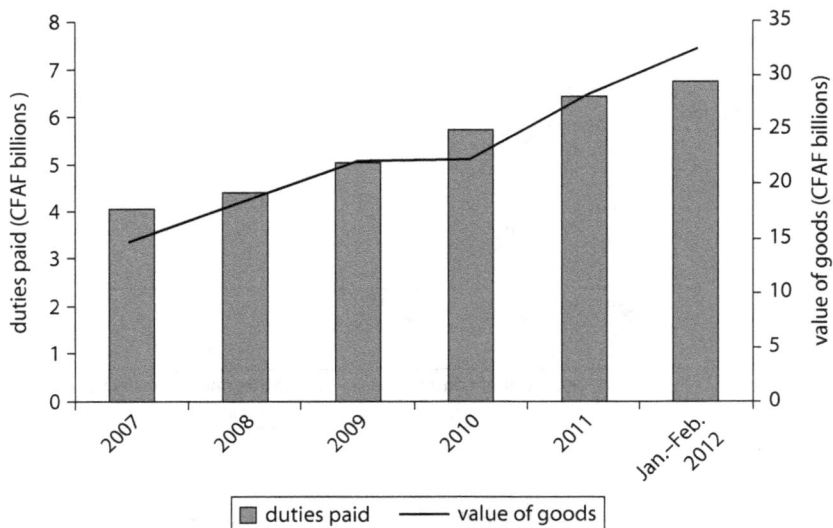

Source: Cameroon Customs information system.

This chapter has set out the difficulties of promoting and controlling the culture of results within a public authority such as Cameroon Customs. Despite internal and external resistance, the General Directorate of Customs has always gone to great lengths to pursue implementation of reforms. Between 2005 and 2011, customs revenues rose from CFAF 345 billion to CFAF 550 billion, a significant jump of CFAF 205 billion and almost 60 percent in current value. Since 2008, the targets set for customs revenue collection have been achieved and exceeded: 104 percent in 2008, 101 percent in 2009, and 103 percent in 2010, cash basis.

The customs administration is not resting on its laurels. The solutions that have made these results possible are the fruit of a process of internal change. However, the venture into performance is something that requires the active involvement of all parties. The process followed by Cameroon Customs is based on a step-by-step approach and is fundamentally empirical in that it is not part of a strategic plan in the process of implementation. In general terms, as previously noted, these initiatives are based on lessons drawn from experience in earlier stages.

Broadly, three aspects of the performance indicators and contracts fostered commitment. First, the indicators and contracts strengthened professional distinctiveness. Sociologists have studied professional distinctiveness in depth. It is the way in which a profession or trade distinguishes itself from others. The performance policy enhanced the value of technical terminology by incorporating it into contracts. It established a common terminology for tables and graphs (Cantens and others 2011a, 2011b). It also introduced some new professional procedures, such as publication of performance reports and performance meetings. Professional associations of customs officers have taken ownership of this change, describing it as giving the profession a new direction. This new, modern direction is key to enhancing professionalism and distinguishing customs officers from police officers, gendarmes, and soldiers, with whom they used to share the reputation of being a corrupt profession.

The second point fostering commitment to professional culture is that the contracts give numerical benchmarks for existing practices. Individual targets are not set by using external data but by using the median figures for the previous three years. The targets therefore take account of existing practices and the rules and standards in force to move them forward. The targets are therefore realistic and acceptable.

The third point fostering commitment is that the contracts enhance the structural autonomy of customs officers. Indeed, like all public servants responsible for enforcement, customs officers have a margin of discretion in their daily work to decide whether to examine something and, in some cases, to determine the severity of any penalty. The contracts acknowledge that individual autonomy while establishing a framework for its application. The inspectors themselves say that the contracts provide a framework for their work and guidance that gives an operational structure.

The performance policy has not, therefore, caused turmoil in customs officers' professional culture; instead it is based on the underlying fabric of that culture—professional distinctiveness, practical rules, and autonomy—and has strengthened it. These structural conditions go a long way toward explaining the success of recent years. They are necessary to the longevity of performance policy, but they are not sufficient in themselves.

The battle is not yet fully won, however, and two important observations are worthy of note. The introduction of performance indicators in 2008 improved quality of service, but then customs reached a plateau. There were indications in 2010 that the same thing might be happening with the contracts. No regression has occurred, but there has been stagnation. Almost all inspectors have attained 100 percent of their targets since that date, and those targets have been amended in view of performance.

To maintain this momentum, Cameroon Customs will have to tackle some major challenges, all of which represent an extension of the reform's scope. First, in contrast to almost all the countries that introduced performance measurement over 10 years ago, Cameroon does not have a centralized, specialist structure responsible for standardizing and invigorating performance policy across all authorities. Customs is the innovator in this field in Cameroon, and it will therefore fall to customs to keep the internal dialogue alive.

The contracts have been extended to new offices and even to economic operators. Nonetheless, internal discussion alone would be a perilous exercise. Performance measurement is a technique that can obscure the political issues concealed in public action. The broadest possible participation is necessary in the debate about what customs performance means in Cameroon, and that participation must involve political authorities and importers. Cameroon Customs has a Customs-Business Forum that should provide a setting for that debate. Finally, this customs reform has encouraged several stakeholders in ports to produce figures themselves. This trend has been seen for a few months and will continue to be positive unless it becomes a vehicle for pitting one set of figures against another. It is therefore in everyone's interest for customs to produce figures together with other stakeholders rather than in competition with one another.

Notes

1. It must be recognized that this approach was an evocation and a misapplication of the concept developed by Peter Drucker. For him, the essence of MBO is the participative way of setting goals. Ideally, when employees themselves have been involved in setting goals and choosing actions, they are more likely to fulfill their responsibilities.

2. ASYCUDA (which stands for Automated System for Customs Data) is a customs clearance computer program developed by the United Nations Conference for Trade and Development and is currently in use in almost 90 countries.

3. The term *partner professions* refers to authorized customs brokers, consignees and carriers, and stevedores, all of whom have a part to play in the customs clearance procedure.

4. There are three color-coded channels. Goods in the red channel require physical inspection. Goods in the yellow channel are subject to document control. Goods in the blue channel are released without immediate customs control but subject to deferred document control.

5. *Reroute* means to redirect the declaration to a processing channel other than the original channel.

6. The Douala Port I customs office deals with goods that are loaded in containers and imported for national consumption, except vehicles. The Douala Port V customs office deals with vehicles imported for national consumption, even those loaded in containers. The Douala external warehouses customs office deals with goods in less-than-container-load containers that are imported for national consumption.

7. All the amounts are in CFAF (Communauté Financière Africaine, or African Financial Community francs) which is the currency used in Cameroon. The conversion rate is €1 = CFAF 655.957.

8. Time scales are calculated from the registration of the manifest to the removal report for goods from the Douala Port.

References

Cantens, Thomas. 2007. "La réforme de la douane camerounaise à l'aide d'un logiciel des Nations unies ou l'approbation d'un outil de finances publiques." *Afrique Contemporaine* 223–224 (3–4): 289–307.

———. 2009. "Etre chef dans les douanes camerounaises, entre ideal type, titular chief et big katika." *Afrique Contemporaine* 230 (2): 83–100.

Cantens, Thomas, Gaël Raballand, Samson Bilangna, and Marcellin Djeuwo. 2011a. "Contracting in Customs Administrations and Its Effects on Corruption and Bad Practices: The Case of Cameroon Customs. Presentation given in Clermont-Ferrand, France, on October 24, 2011, during the conference on tax and development held by the Centre d'Études et de Recherches sur le Développement International and the International Centre for Tax and Development in Clermont-Ferrand, France, October 24.

———. 2011b. "Reforming Customs by Measuring Performance: A Cameroon Case Study." In *Where to Spend the Next Million? Applying Impact Evaluation to Trade Assistance*, ed. Olivier Cadot, Ana M. Fernandes, Julien Gourdon, and Aaditya Mattoo, 183–206. Washington, DC: World Bank.

Cartier-Bresson, Jean. 2008. *Économie politique de la corruption et de la gouvernance*. Paris: L'Harmattan.

Drucker, Peter F. (1954) 2007. *The Practice of Management*. Oxford, U.K.: Elsevier.

Libom Li Likeng, Minette, Thomas Cantens, and Samson Bilangna. 2009. "Gazing into the Mirror: Operational Internal Controls in Cameroon Customs." Regional Integration and Transport Discussion Paper 8, Sub-Saharan Africa Transport Policy Program, World Bank, Washington, DC.

Libom Li Likeng, Minette, Marcellin Djeuwo, and Samson Bilangna. 2011. "Gazing into the Mirror II: Performance Contracts in Cameroon Customs." Good Practice Paper 1, Sub-Saharan Africa Transport Policy Program, World Bank, Washington, DC.

Plane, Jean-Michel. 2003. *Management des organisations: Théories, concepts, cas.* Paris: Dunod.

CHAPTER 3

The Revenue Imperative in Cameroon

Administrative Dilemmas

José-María Muñoz

"If the tax authorities had provided us with figures, this would have helped us understand. Tax revenues have fallen. Yes, okay. But to what extent?" The prefect of the Vina district (Adamaoua, Cameroon) asked this question during a meeting in Ngaoundéré, Cameroon, on September 10, 2004. It was one of the rare instances I witnessed in which taxpayers encountered tax officials and other local representatives of the government for a thorough discussion of specific tax-related issues.[1] As the meeting went on, the prefect's sympathy for the tax administration's attempt at more rigorous enforcement faded into growing impatience with the administration's reticence to provide precise collection figures. That numbers, or rather their absence, surfaced as a matter of concern in this meeting revealed the broader context of public administration reform in Cameroon, which, following prevalent global trends, espoused numbers as the privileged tool to appraise and foster administrative performance. This chapter explores an iconic component of that larger reform effort, the tax administration's experiment in performance-based management that was launched in 2002 under the name *direction par objectifs* (DPO, or management by objectives).

The analytical and methodological inspiration of this chapter comes largely from the anthropology of policy and bureaucracy. That literature has identified accountability as shorthand for a new phenomenon with long-standing moral and financial credentials (Strathern 2000). The practices that the mantra of accountability has generated within organizations in the most diverse places and domains play determining roles in the allocation of resources across the world. These audit cultures, with their distinctive language and their constant redefinition of what counts and what does not, have become sources of aspiration and anxiety in a variety of contexts in both southern and northern countries (Shore, Wright, and Pero 2011). I also draw additional insights from Douglas Holmes's (2009) research on the development of monetary policy by central banks in New Zealand and elsewhere. Holmes emphasizes the experimental ethos that permeates the process of developing policy models and sustaining them through time. He invites researchers to pay attention to "the continuous evolution of a set of social practices" as well as "the critical labor" by which personnel of organizations modify the assumptions that inform policy initiatives as they unfold (Holmes 2009, 386–87).

The particular policy ideas that inspired DPO involved relying on quantitative measures of performance as the main tool for making personnel accountable. Numbers are particularly appealing technologies of power in that the objectivity and neutrality widely granted to them appear to set them apart from political interests, above the world of factional intrigue, and beyond debate (Porter 1995). One is therefore well advised to see in the numbers collected and used within the DPO framework a significance that goes beyond the task for which those figures are deployed. Numbers are normative in that not only do they push members of an organization to meet targets, but also they take for granted a certain statistical infrastructure and call for those actors' systematic scrutiny of particular aspects of their activities (Anders 2008). Along those lines, critical accounting studies have called attention to the fact that calculative practices are not simply instrumental and reflective but also constitutive. Tools like DPO are adopted for "their ability to translate diverse and complex processes into a single financial figure" (Miller 2001, 381). However, once adopted, they set in motion a series of potentially transformative dynamics. The success of those translations depends on laborious assemblages of people, things, and ideas (Latour 1996). DPO is no exception in this regard.

Tax administration has long been considered a particularly fertile ground for management accounting. Since the 1960s, Nicholas Kaldor's

(1963, 417) classic formulation that revenue authorities offered a "point of entry" for civil service reform has remained the conventional wisdom on these matters. This canonical policy vision had two key ingredients: on the one hand, revenue offered a straightforward measure of performance; on the other hand, revenue itself was a strong incentive to improve performance. In revenue departments, as Alex Radian (1980, 16) put it, "money makes money." The task of appraising efficiency and effectiveness on the basis of revenue has nonetheless proved daunting. Today, most experts would agree with Richard Bird (2004, 135) that "assessing the relation between administrative effort and revenue outcome is by no means a simple task" (see also Raffinot 2001). What is more, as Bird also notes (and as critics of Cameroonian DPO have tried to assert in the past decade), maximizing revenue is only one dimension of the task of tax administration. As this chapter will show, the evolving design of DPO has had a hard time coming to grips with the knowledge that "revenue outcomes may not always be the most appropriate basis for assessing administrative performance" (Bird 2004, 135).

These long-held notions about the potential of revenue to serve as a yardstick of performance were only strengthened in the era of new public management (NPM) reforms. The ideas and ideals that animated this "public management for all seasons," as Christopher Hood (1991) aptly characterized it, need little rehearsing here. But the research agenda that calls for an analysis of the elaboration of NPM's principles in particular settings and their interaction with the calculative instruments that seek to make them operational has not lost any of its currency (Kurunmäki, Lapsley, and Miller 2011). This chapter contributes to that collective effort.

Raoul Tamekou (2008, 243) has written that "Cameroon has inscribed itself resolutely in the NPM's trajectory." It is an assertion that needs to be tempered—as Tamekou himself does when he warns that "the ink is still fresh" and many components of the reforms are still "at project stage"—but that nonetheless gives a sense of the resources and people that NPM has mobilized in the country in the past two decades. The contour of Cameroonian initiatives to reform public administration, which owes much to conditions contained in the government's agreements with the World Bank and the International Monetary Fund, can only be sketched here. The early years of structural adjustment were spent in half-hearted attempts at reducing the state payroll through layoffs and salary cuts. The scope of reform was broadened in 1994 with the introduction of a new legal framework aimed at improving civil service standards and relations with the citizenry.[2] While the new statute for state employees proclaimed the need to constantly assess performance, the mechanisms of assessment and the system of rewards and penalties remained unspecified (Ngouo 1997). The customs and tax authorities' DPO formulas were, in fact, the first (and to date the most noteworthy) attempts to specify those mechanisms. Since 1994, numerous government initiatives tackling different aspects of the state organizational structure and procedures have seen the light, most of them placed under the mantle of the "good governance" agenda.[3] Drawing from the repertoire of managerial formulas that are in vogue, most of these programs have attracted generous funding from a series of donors, including the United Nations Development Programme, the World Bank, the European Union, Canada, and France. They have mobilized the energies of foreign and national consultants (Ngouo 2000); found ministerial departments or factions within them particularly receptive to the opportunities that these initiatives offered (Ngouo 2008); and fizzled out in due course as the networks, interests, and devices that they brought together lost consistency. As suggested by Béatrice Hibou (2006, 297) in her work on the Tunisian regime, one should not discard the possibility that these "reforms in perpetuity" are what constitute the "success of reformism." Be that as it may, learning to coexist with reform has become part of the social condition of Cameroonian civil servants.

Cameroon's Experiment in Management by Objectives

Although Cameroonian tax authorities nominally espoused the DPO formula in the mid-1990s, its adoption did not materialize until the following decade and only after what an inside critic has called "a period of equivocation" (Evina Obam 2005, 20). This tentative and protracted start-up underscored what has remained one of the enduring traits of the Cameroonian DPO formula—its experimental quality. This experimental quality was also prominent when senior government officials presented DPO to the public. Thus, when in 1999 the minister of economy and finance summed up for the benefit of the National Assembly's Fiscal Commission the main reforms undertaken in the fiscal domain, he described what had taken place within the tax administration as "the experimentation of management by objectives" (quoted in Atanga Fongue 2007, 55). Accordingly, it seems fitting to think of DPO as a "work in progress" (see Holmes 2009, 308).

DPO is the French translation of the English management by objectives (MBO), a concept made popular in the 1950s by the Austrian-American management expert Peter Drucker (1954). Although MBO recipes were advocated as a way to organize the public sector as early as the 1930s, the idea did not gain broad acceptance until the 1960s (Drucker 1976). In the United States, 1973 marked a watershed in this regard, because it was over the course of this year that the Nixon administration introduced MBO as one of the key means of managing federal agencies and programs (Dirsmith and Jablonsky 1979). In France, as early as the 1960s, management specialists such as Octave Gélinier had already taken it on themselves to bear Drucker's torch. Although Gélinier set his sights largely on the French private sector (Boltanski and Chiapello 2005, 69), the influence of his ideas, which were voiced in a quick succession of influential publications (Gélinier 1965, 1966, 1968), was also felt by the national public sector (Chaty 1997). As Siwek-Pouydesseau (1974) documented at the time, Gélinier's indefatigable advocacy ended up instigating a spirited debate on the suitability of private management formulas for state bureaucracies and inspiring the first ministerial experiments with DPO and its offshoot DPPO (*direction participative par objectifs*, or participatory management by objectives).

I am not in a position to speculate about what may have pushed the Cameroonian authorities to opt for the French idiosyncratic version of a formula that was initially developed by U.S. experts in business administration several decades earlier. The judiciousness of such a choice has certainly been questioned in Cameroon on the grounds that DPO was, by the 1990s, an already outdated designation (Evina Obam 2005, 55, n. 51). By that time, France had already embarked on an ambitious and far-reaching project of modernizing its public administration through two waves of measures (1989–92 and 1995–97), which had been decided by the prime ministers during those periods, Michel Rocard and Alain Juppé, respectively (Clark 1998; Guyomarch 1999). In its sui generis and piecemeal adoption of NPM recipes, France had adopted a renewed vocabulary in which the DPO formula had no place. It is also unclear how much weight these genealogical connections—which incidentally are not uncommon in the broader landscape of Cameroon's law and administration—had on the decisions of those who conceived and subsequently reworked Cameroon's DPO. In any case, the results of transferring this foreign technology to Cameroon should not be thought of as having somehow been prefigured in the technology's earlier trajectory. The place of Cameroon in the global political economy and the country's relationships with key financial partners matter in this and other aspects of the country's administrative reform. Yet what DPO has come to be in Cameroon today also reflects the state's organizational patterns and repertoires of action, as well as the evolving shape of tax compliance.

What then has the DPO label stood for in Cameroon in recent years? From its earliest incarnation, DPO has come to designate a series of procedures through which the tax units receive targets that function as yardsticks for appraising their performance. This vague characterization is no accident. As Roland Evina Obam (2005, 12) explains, "No legal instrument making explicit [DPO's] content has been formally issued, much less an internal handbook in the manner of a guide allowing officials a better grasp of the system." Nonetheless, these lacunae have not prevented DPO from becoming a central concern in the everyday operation of the tax administration.

That DPO is today on everyone's lips at tax centers around the country is no minor achievement. In my interviews with tax officials, references to DPO surface regularly: "For a *chef de centre* [head of tax center] it is the fulfillment rate of their DPO that becomes critical"; "The [value added tax] is our *produit haut de gamme* [top-quality product]. It represents more than a third of our DPO"; "The provincial head of taxes evaluates all the centers in the province on the basis of them doing their DPO. And he can be a tough judge!" Those and similar remarks often struck me for their ambivalence. On one hand, the words were uttered with a touch of pride. Not only did these officials carry out their work with utmost zeal, but they also had something to show for it in the form of revenue. This line of reasoning often drew an implicit contrast with the much maligned mores of other branches of the Cameroonian civil service, not unlike the contrast Evina Obam (2005, 24) draws explicitly in the following quote: "In the Cameroonian administration as a whole, the *Direction Générale des Impôts* [Directorate General of Taxation] is unique in having firmly and irreversibly embarked on the hazardous road to performance-based management." As an official once told me when discussing DPO, "We are no ordinary [public] administration." As Strathern (2006, 188) has suggested when writing about "new accountabilities" in the United Kingdom, the awe experienced by the officials who learn how the DPO is "done" is also an "awe of technique." As this British anthropologist has eloquently written, from the perspective of the actors involved, what these accountability mechanisms generate is "not just a depiction of ourselves produced in order to impress others but a picture that shows how impressed we are with ourselves." On the other hand, as Evina Obam's reference to the hazards along the road intimates, my informants' professional pride when talking about DPO was frequently tinged with trepidation. Revenue objectives had subjected these officials to unprecedented pressures, which were magnified by their inability to influence either the targets being set or the extraneous factors that determined their success in attaining those targets.

Dealing in Numbers

DPO not only is talked about; it also is carried out. It is a task that requires continuous attention and a task whose demands are heightened periodically. Its rhythm is a function of two parallel dynamics. The first one derives from the features of the tax system, which subjects taxpayers to a series of obligations that have to be performed according to specified schedules. Different taxes involve different calendars. Different categories of taxpayers face obligations to report and pay that differ in substance and frequency. These aspects have an obvious effect on the pace at which revenue is collected. The second dynamic affecting the operation of DPO is instituted by the principles that structure the work of the different units that make up the Cameroonian tax administration. Both dynamics suffered momentous transformations during the years when DPO became operational. Not only did substantial changes to the tax system take place "halfway through the year, without previous notice, through a decree or an ordinance, depending on budgetary constraints," but also the tax administration's shifting configuration made officials often feel as if they were "groping in the dark" (Alaka Alaka 2009, 39, 49).[4]

As far as DPO is concerned, a cycle begins every year with the announcement of the revenue targets. A series of periodic monitoring exercises proceed until the cycle closes by the end of the year with an evaluation of the results achieved. That evaluation feeds into the setting of revised targets for the following year. Once targets are decided globally, each unit is assigned the portion of revenue for which it will be held accountable. Thus, at the regional level, the regional heads allocate the share of the collection effort for each tax center under their authority. The heads of the subordinate centers, in turn, proceed to break down those figures into revenue quotas for which their staffs should answer. In the professional jargon, this process is referred to as *saucissonage* (chopping up), and it leads to a *DPO personnalisée* (personalized DPO); that is, both tax centers and the members of staff within them have assigned targets (Pekassa Ndam 2010).

The monitoring of progress in attaining targets takes place at regular coordination meetings. At the regional level, the results are scrutinized in weekly meetings and sent to the Directorate General of Taxation (Direction Générale des Impôts, or DGI). At the national level, monthly meetings take place at the DGI's headquarters in Yaoundé. These meetings and monitoring practices presuppose the gathering of data and the generation of statistics by tax centers. This assembly of data has not been achieved overnight. If numbers are to become normative standards, an infrastructure of systematic data collection needs to be in place (see Anders 2008). When in the mid-1990s the Cameroonian tax authorities officially embraced DPO as their key operating principle, basic ingredients of this infrastructure, such as computerization and a trained staff, were missing in most tax centers.[5]

I witnessed the process of making such an infrastructure operative during my first stay in Cameroon between June 2003 and November 2004. I had traveled to Adamaoua, one of the country's three northern provinces, within the framework of a research project on the two pillars of the provincial economy: the cattle and transport sectors. Over the course of my visits to the provincial tax services in the city of Ngaoundéré and my conversations with the staff members, I realized to what extent the routines of DPO were still by and large regarded as novelties. "We are now compelled to deliver in terms of results, somewhat like the private [sector]," a senior official told me in one of my first formal interviews before he went on to vent some of the frustrations brought on by his attempts to instill this "philosophy" in his subordinates. I still have a vivid recollection of a morning in October 2004, when the official in charge of statistics at the provincial services patiently walked me through the data of the past two years. When I asked about earlier records, I was assured that before 2002 (the year when DPO became operational) the way statistics were kept was chaotic. So that I could see for myself that the provincial tax administration was in "a situation of almost total obscurity," the obliging official took the trouble of showing me a couple of annual statistical summaries from the late 1990s.

By 2004, all provincial tax services were in a position to provide the Directorate of Taxes (Direction des Impôts), the predecessor of the DGI, with weekly and monthly figures on things such as revenue figures by type of tax, overdue sums pending collection, and fulfillment rate of DPO by tax center. Equipped with those numbers, the provincial (later regional) heads would then travel to Yaoundé every month to answer for the performance of the tax centers under their supervision. In such meetings, DPO became the object of assessment by the director general and his team. A senior official at the DGI, who spoke from his years of experience as regional head, elaborated on the vulnerability of their position: "It is every month. You find yourself sitting across the table from the director. The management indicators, the performance report, and the action plan are there for everyone to see. . . . The job of regional head is tough!" Some officials are commended; others are reprimanded. Those in charge of regions that have failed to come up with the goods have the most justifying and convincing to do. Why such figures? What corrective measures are envisaged? What militates in favor of revising the targets downward? These are some of the recurrent questions. If regional heads have considerable maneuvering room in justifying departures from assigned targets, it is precisely because the relationship between the administrative effort and the revenue outcome that DPO posits is anything but straightforward.

Consider again the case of Adamaoua's tax administration in 2004. The creation of the Large Business Office (Direction des Grandes Entreprises, or DGE) the year before had meant that the files of the seven largest businesses based in the province had been transferred to Yaoundé.[6] This is what the head of the provincial services had to say about this change: "The departure of those enterprises has had an enormous impact on our revenue. As a matter of fact, since it is all now centralized in Yaoundé, it makes no difference. So we are told. But, I say to myself, Adamaoua has suffered as a result. Our revenue has dropped greatly." The loss of its most important taxpayers to a newly created administrative unit had naturally been reflected in Adamaoua's targets for 2004. All the same, the provincial head of taxes had found a powerful justification for Adamaoua's failure to meet the revised targets in the shortcomings of these estimates. As he explained, "We hadn't really measured the impact [of the creation of the DGE]. Our calculations resulted from extrapolating what we collected from these enterprises. It's only after the fact that we've understood there were also other large enterprises with headquarters outside Adamaoua, which used to pay numerous taxes and fees here and they don't anymore." He had made this point clear in coordination meetings in Yaoundé in the early months of 2004. In a case like this one, the authorities in Yaoundé might be inclined to show understanding, among other reasons because the stakes are relatively low. Adamaoua's administration today collects less than 0.5 percent of the country's total tax revenue.[7]

With time, as DPO has become a routine element of tax officials' work, some tax centers seem to have succeeded in neutralizing its destabilizing potential. In my recent conversations with officials at the East's regional tax center, for example, the mood was one of confidence in their ability to stay safely above the assigned targets. The global numbers of this regional tax center in recent years tell a story of steady progress in mobilizing revenue.[8] A more careful examination of which units within the center and which tax categories revenue came from complicates such a stylized story. For example, changes in tax law during the past three years have seriously affected revenue generated by the value added tax (by suppressing and then reinstating this tax's withholding mechanism). The ups and downs of value added tax collection have been compensated by the higher or lower productivity of other taxes. Similarly, disappointing results of some tax units in the region have been offset by higher than average results in other units. Officials still characterize the balancing acts involved in achieving the aggregate targets as ranging from "laborious" to "extremely challenging." Overall, however, by now officials such as these have, if not perfected the DPO experiment, at least domesticated it.

Justifications for insufficient collection figures matter because they preempt harsh treatment by superiors along the hierarchical chain on which DPO relies. This observation should also draw attention to the discretion that presides in decisions over not only the setting of targets but also the consequences of recurrent underperformance. In recent years, a few sporadic cases of exemplary measures have caught a modicum of media attention. In November 2004, for example, the minister of finance and budget suspended seven heads of tax centers in Yaoundé and Douala for insufficient performance (Chendjou 2004). About a year later, the disciplinary suspensions reached higher up, affecting some 20 officials in charge of audits at the DGI. Their faults were once more related to insufficient performance (Mbodiam 2005). However, in such rare instances, signs of the increased importance of performance-based logic are difficult to see. Rather, these cases tend to be explained away in terms of factional fights within the tax administration. Their episodic nature, in any case, speaks of the absence of an established system of penalties for poor performance.

Under the Sway of the Revenue Imperative

What has been said so far makes apparent that in Cameroon, DPO, a system conceived to assess the contributions of individuals working for an organization, has been reduced to a numerical target. The series of met-onymical operations that tax officials perform when they talk about meeting the demands of the system are eloquent in this regard. Consider the excerpts from my field notes that I quoted above: "the fulfillment rate of their DPO"; "[the value added tax] represents more than a third of our DPO"; "doing their DPO." In this miniature sample, what is referred to as DPO is either the revenue target set for a given period or the revenue collected in attaining such a target. For these officials, "doing their DPO" means collecting a sum of money. As one of them put it, their objectives are measured *"en espèces sonantes et trébuchantes"* (in cold, hard cash).

Notionally, DPO in Cameroon has from its inception referred to both quantitative and qualitative objectives. However, the qualitative objectives, the methods to assess them, and the incentives to give them traction remained at first completely unspecified. The almost exclusive focus not only on quantitative objectives but also on revenue targets more precisely probably had a lot to do with their apparent simplicity. These targets provided a sense of purpose for all units within the tax administration at a time when the World Bank and the International Monetary Fund were warning Cameroon about the urgency of mobilizing nonoil revenue.[9] Indeed, it did not take long for the overhaul in tax policy and administration that followed the fiscal reform of 1995 to affect nonoil revenue figures (AfDB 2008; Evina Obam 2005; Fambon 2006).

Within the tax administration, the first critical voices against this almost exclusive focus on revenue objectives came from the ranks of officials responsible for assessing compliance and conducting audits. The first attempt to specify the implications of performance-based management for controllers and auditors had been an instruction issued by the national director of taxes in early 2002. This instruction stipulated that every year tax centers should subject to verification at least a fourth of the taxpayer registry. Furthermore, each official was individually assigned a minimum number of verifications per year. Moreover, the contribution of the tax controllers to the revenue raised by the tax center of which they were part was expected to amount to at least 10 percent of the center's DPO.

The contents of this 2002 instruction aroused a wave of objections, which Roland Atanga Fongue (2007, 54–57) aptly summed up. The instruction set objectives across the board that failed to reflect the diverse situations faced by the control services in different tax centers, in which the ratio of taxpayers to officials varies widely. Most critics questioned the rationale of setting revenue targets for the services responsible for control and auditing. Most considered the method too blunt an instrument to assess and orient the auditors' work. Did the logic of revenue maximization not pose a threat to key goals of control, such as the fight against fraud and the equal treatment of taxpayers? Why link the objectives of audit services to the revenue targets of production services? Why set a seemingly arbitrary 10 percent, when there are audit services that achieve "their annual objectives in six months while others have not reached a fourth of their objectives by the end of the year" (Atanga Fongue 2007, 56)?

In any case, the means to enforce the objectives set by the 2002 instruction remained vague and inadequate. That is why, incidentally, the auditors and controllers who were suspended in November 2005, on the grounds that they had not reached a fifth of their revenue targets, felt the stated reason was only an excuse (Mbodiam 2005). Improvements to the existing system for monitoring the work of controllers and auditors have proved hard to obtain. As a new instruction issued on January 3, 2008, acknowledged in its preamble, there persist "shortcomings in the monitoring and assessment of operational units, most notably the absence of real indicators measuring the effectiveness of controls, auditing action plans, and monthly numerical performance reports in those units."[10] In its closing lines, the instruction announced the elaboration of specific indicators for these tax officials, which to my knowledge has not materialized to this day (Pekassa Ndam 2010).

As far as the provincial tax services responsible for processing returns and collecting taxes are concerned, it was paradoxically a drop in nonoil revenue in 2002 and 2003 that nurtured the calls for superseding the reliance on revenue targets as the main organizing principle of their activity. A process that Evina Obam (2005, 34) characterizes as an internal debate led the Ministry of Finance to "gradually refine the measuring tools" and broaden the range of performance indicators. At that time, statistical services in provincial tax centers began reporting on indicators such as numbers of newly registered taxpayers and recovery rates of tax arrears pending payment. At the provincial and district levels, such indicators could offer the tax centers a way out of the conundrum of having to answer for often arbitrary revenue targets that might prove to be beyond their reach. For Adamaoua province's tax services, for example, the new indicators were very important in 2004. This was a period when, as a result of the creation of the DGE and the completion of the Chad-Cameroon pipeline, the head of the provincial tax administration was presiding over dwindling revenue figures. This situation had pushed him, he explained, to instill added impetus to the tax services' efforts to enlarge the taxpaying base, a goal that was likely to yield meager revenue outcomes but for which he was given credit in the Directorate of Taxes' managerial plan for that year.

This gradual transition toward the incorporation of management indicators culminated in the director general's instruction of July 22, 2005, on performance monitoring, which formally integrated the indicators in the DPO template. However, participants in the system believe that top decision makers give negligible weight to nonrevenue indicators even to this day. A recent conversation with a senior official at the East region's tax services offers a good illustration.[11] He was discussing the difficulties he had witnessed in relations between the customs and the tax administration as well as those between different units within the tax administration. He regretted the time and energy he had to spend requesting from other centers or departments key information about taxpayers who fell within his jurisdiction, often to no avail. As he explained,

> When you depend on somebody else [to gather information], your concerns always come second. Those other people are going to have other priorities. Reaching their objectives is their priority. Until further notice, for us, it's all about figures. Qualitative indicators are nowhere to be found, no matter what we tell ourselves. We are centered on quantitative objectives. Put yourself in the shoes of the blokes at the DGE. If they got [CFAF] 50 billion last year, this year they want to make this other amount. . . . If the transmission of information counted as an indicator of the quality of our work, perhaps that would help others reach their quantitative objectives.

His statement is a reminder that in the present system officials get no recognition or reward for sharing information with their colleagues, nor are they censored or punished for their failure to do so. His line of reasoning is not that distant from the one that inspired the redesign of DPO in 2005, which gained a foothold after revenue improvements had hit a wall. The exclusive reliance on crude measures to assess the work of tax officials had a long-term detrimental impact on revenue. Rewarding a measure of performance that encourages the single-minded, short-term maximization of revenue makes officials neglect aspects of their work that have an indirect but tangible effect on revenue itself. The system may divert the tax administration from the path toward increased efficiency and effectiveness. It is as if, in the seas of tax administration, the Cameroonian authorities had chosen to stay inshore rather than go fishing in deep waters.

Performance-Based Management at the Taxpaying Interface

This last section explores the possibility that DPO not only provides the manifest framework for decision making within the tax administration but also is used to present the tax administration's actions to the public. In this light, management by numbers involves a dimension of communication that is predicated on the circulation of a new vocabulary around revenue outcomes. The views expressed by the DGE's director in an interview with the government newspaper give a sense of this generative aspect of DPO:

> In its role as laboratory for the segmentation of the taxpaying population, the DGE should bind itself to the standards of the New Public Management through the diffusion of best practices in a global management environment that is experiencing deep transformations. Cameroon is today equipped with a new financial regime and a program to modernize its public administration through results-based management. The *direction par objectifs* makes tax officials adapt themselves, as public service workers, [to these shifts] by becoming true experts. Competent, accessible, proactive, receptive and creative, they must break with the customary logic governed by the resources at their disposal in favor of a logic of results, thus benefiting the collectivity and the taxpayers (Foute 2008).

These words aptly capture the tenor of public statements by senior officials in the tax administration in recent years. The administration's emphasis on modernization and experimentation, which the metaphor of the laboratory evokes powerfully; the acknowledgment of the need to respond to global transformations; and the reference to the notion of public service rather than *puissance publique*, its less pleasant counterpart, have become platitudes in present-day Cameroon. All the same, the quote is interesting because it makes explicit the transformative effect that DPO has on tax officials and the way they approach their work. The metamorphosis of officials that DPO demands has an effect on taxpayers and society at large—a beneficial one, according to the DGE director's predisposed views. What kind of pedagogy underlies statements such as this one? Such statements are not aimed at informing the public about the targets set or the degree of fulfillment of those targets. Instead they seem to be instances of what Luc Sindjoun (1996, 65) has in a related context called "the dramatization of technocratic and legal-rational discourse." They only gesture at the numerical components of DPO and their effects. In media appearances such as the government newspaper interview, actual numbers are only rarely displayed and then only as rough figures casually thrown out.

The words of the Vina district's prefect, quoted in the opening paragraph of this chapter, are again relevant: "If the tax authorities had provided us with figures. . . ." Their immediate context was a conflict that arose in September 2004 between the tax authorities and cattle merchants in Adamaoua province's wealthiest district. The merchants perceived these tensions as directly resulting from the pressures placed on the provincial tax services to meet their revenue targets. In correspondence addressed to the railway company, which is entrusted with collecting advances of the cattle merchants' income tax when they load cattle, the national director of taxes had singled out the merchants' evasion as being responsible for a significant drop in collection figures. A meeting was organized to find a way out of the ensuing stalemate.

I found one aspect of this meeting particularly striking at the time: how intractable the task of putting a number to the decrease in revenue under discussion proved to be. Early in the meeting, the prefect, who presided over the meeting, invited the head of the district tax center to furnish a precise amount. In successive exchanges, the head of the district tax center chose to leave this request unanswered. Only when hard pressed by the prefect for the umpteenth time did he volunteer a number: "Here and now, it would be difficult for us to venture a figure. All that can be said is that, after careful study, the cattle sector in the province should yield around a billion and seven hundred thousand francs." Of tax revenue? asked the prefect. "Yes, of tax revenue." Annually? asked the prefect again. "Yes, annually." Although the prefect was visibly struck by how substantial this estimate of potential tax revenue was, it was still not the number he had asked for.

More than an hour later, after the meeting had taken a frustrating turn for the tax authorities, the head of the district tax center finally heeded the prefect's request and gave a figure of revenue actually realized: "If I take the situation of the district, the monthly revenue objective that has been set for us is sixty million [francs]. This is the revenue we should raise. Last month, that is August 2004, we have only made twenty-two million. Note that the government is making estimations relying on your [the merchants'] contribution and that you have not paid your part." Much to the disappointment of everyone present, this was as much information as he was prepared to release. The answer referred to the gap between assigned targets and revenue for only one month, and it offered no term of comparison, such as the revenue raised in that month in previous years. The prefect had to make do with such unsatisfactory ingredients to keep his mediation efforts alive.[12]

Examples such as this one demonstrate that the taxpayers' awareness of the new pressures that govern the operations of tax centers throughout the country is matched by the reticence of tax officials to divulge those targets to the people from whom they are collecting taxes. Until recently, sharing revenue figures has not been part of the tax authorities' often-invoked mission to educate taxpayers, which is today one of the cornerstones of the new tax administration–taxpayer partnership. In places like Adamaoua, this disavowal of transparency feeds taxpayers' suspicions that a portion of the money collected ends up in the pockets of officials and others involved in the collection process rather than in the national treasury—which was indeed one of the conclusions cattle merchants drew from the episode just recounted. In my research experience, the tax administration's educational efforts tend to limit themselves to reminders and clarifications of the constantly shifting rules governing matters such as administrative procedures, reporting obligations, or taxpaying categories and rates.

Yet if the Cameroonian tax authorities have so far been content to build their partnership with taxpayers by and large through the formalist reiteration of the changing letter of the law, there have been some attempts to go beyond a pedagogy premised on "the suspicion and stigmatization of taxpayers" (Atanga Fongue 2007, 14). Thus, in recent years, several tax centers have organized press conferences to publicize their collection figures. The Littoral region's Tax Center 1, for example, presented its 2010 annual report in February 3, 2011 (Endong 2011). During such public events, heads of tax centers discuss in detail trends in numbers of different categories of taxpayers and the relative importance of different taxes in terms of revenue. In this, the tax authorities may have drawn lessons from the proactive media strategy adopted by the country's customs administration, discussed by Bilangna and Djeuwo in chapter 2. However, hitherto these events have been isolated and have yet to become established institutional practice. As in the customs case, these efforts have also been largely restricted to tax centers where the revenue stakes are the highest. They are also far from the ambitions of initiatives described in recent ethnographies of tax administration, such as the one deployed by the Argentine Federal Tax Administration in 2005 and 2006, where extensive and high-impact use of the media was combined with performance-based management to redefine the effective dimensions of tax payments (Abelin 2012).

This chapter has offered a characterization of the *direction par objectifs* (management by directives, or DPO), one of the Cameroonian government's iconic attempts to use calculative practices to improve administrative performance. DPO appears to be an experiment that is predicated as much on a series of administrative practices and routines as on the circulation of a new language. The preceding pages have tried to explore DPO's genealogy, the transformations it has introduced in the operation of the tax administration, the rhythms of its hierarchical chain of accountability, and its reliance on revenue as the ultimate determinant of what counts and what needs to be accounted for. At the taxpaying interface, DPO has so far played no significant part in the ongoing debate between tax authorities and taxpayers. Instead, it has been deployed as a symbol of technocratic prowess for the benefit of the country's citizenry and international partners as much as for that of the growing taxpaying population. Ultimately, the trajectory of DPO in Cameroon owes little to the so-called revenue imperative. This is the paradox that this chapter has sought to illuminate. From the vantage point of the present, the DPO experiment, which has had undeniable success in cobbling together a reform program out of key actors and devices for over a decade now, seems to have outlived its usefulness as a tool for technocratic building and expansion.

Notes

1. This chapter relies on ethnographic materials gathered during the author's extended field research in Cameroon from June 2003 to November 2004, and during two more recent research trips (August 2010 and May–June 2011). The author wishes to thank the Cameroonian tax officials who have generously shared their time and views with him over the course of these years. The chapter also draws numerous insights from an expanding corpus of doctoral dissertations and other secondary sources on tax administration in Cameroon. Lotta Björklund-Larsen, a passionate advocate of studying taxes ethnographically, called the author's attention to Douglas Holmes' work on central banks. Giorgio Blundo provided discerning and constructive comments on an earlier version of this chapter. Without the encouragement and determination of Thomas Cantens and Gaël Raballand, these pages would not have been written.

2. The Statut Général de la Fonction Publique de l'Etat, contained in decree 1994/117, of October 7, 1994, was drafted with the United Nations Development Programme's active participation (Bruneau and Abouem 2004).

3. These initiatives include the overarching National Governance Program (the program has had two phases, 2000–04 and 2006–10); the Computer System

for the Integrated Management of State Personnel and Payroll (Système Informatique de Gestion Intégrés des Personnels de l'État et de la Solde, or SIGIPES); a series of administrative procedure handbooks at the ministerial level; the Project for the Introduction of Performance Standards (Projet d'Introduction des Normes de Rendement dans l'Administration Camerounaise, or PINORAC); and the Program for the Modernization of the Administration through Performance-Based Management (Promotion de la Gestion Axée sur les Résultats, or PROMAGAR).

4. The long-standing distinction between central services and decentralized services (*services déconcentrés*) relied on a territorial basis along the lines of Cameroon's administrative grid. In the present constellation, the Cameroonian tax administration is no longer organized in provinces (or regions in more recent times) and districts. The segmentation of the taxpaying population by size has gradually overridden territorial principles (Pekassa Ndam 2010). The Large Business Office (Direction des Grandes Entreprises), the tax centers for medium-size companies (*centres des impôts des moyennes entreprises*), and the divisional tax centers (*centres divisionnaires des impôts*) are now the main building blocks.

5. Both aspects of information processing within the tax administration have been long-term endeavors. The substantial recruitment effort (Evina Obam 2005), both through the National School of Administration and Magistracy (École Nationale d'Administration et de Magistrature) and the consolidation of the positions of temporary agents, has not dissipated two old problems of the tax administration's personnel: (a) the overall low qualifications and inadequate sets of skills and (b) a disproportionate number of managers in relation to frontline officials (Atanga Fongue 2007; Pekassa Ndam 2010). The computerization efforts started in the mid-1980s with a program called TRINITE, which had in the late 1990s a successor called TRINITE II. An initiative to move to a more sophisticated treatment of tax-related information was tried out at the DGI under the name MESURE (Ossa 2007). In 2009, the DGI announced the launching of a plan of general computerization.

6. The DGE was created pursuant to Decree 2003/165 of June 30, 2003.

7. The complaints of the provincial head at the time should be read in this light. He was complaining precisely about the lowering of the stakes that the creation of the DGE had represented.

8. In recent years, the East's regional center has managed to keep pace with increasing targets. In 2009, with an objective of CFAF 3,254,900,000, it collected CFAF 3,347,000,000. In 2010, a target of CFAF 3,518,200,000 was exceeded by CFAF 5,200,000. In 2011, a steep objective of CFAF 4,031,400,000 was matched by a total collection of CFAF 4,289,206,962.

9. This concern was already present in the first studies that the International Monetary Fund's Fiscal Affairs Department conducted on behalf of the

Cameroonian government in 1990 within the framework of the country's structural adjustment program (Nashashibi, Ouanes, and Clawson 1990).

10. The full text of the instruction is available at http://www.impots.cm/uploads/pdf/circulaires/Instruction%20cadre%20controle%202008.pdf.

11. The interview took place in Bertoua, May 26, 2011.

12. For a detailed account of this meeting, see Muñoz (2011).

References

Abelin, Mireille. 2012. "Fiscal Sovereignty: Reconfigurations of Value and Citizenship in Post-financial Crisis Argentina." Doctoral thesis, Columbia University, New York.

AfDB (African Development Bank). 2008. "Republique du Cameroun: Un espace budgetaire renforcé pour la croissance et la réduction de la pauvreté." http://www.afdb.org/fileadmin/uploads/afdb/Documents/Project-and-Operations/30774762-EN-CAMEROUN-UN-ESPACE-BUDGETAIRE-RENFORCE.PDF.

Alaka Alaka, Pierre. 2009. *L'impôt au Cameroun: Contributions à l'étude d'un dysfonctionnement administratif.* Paris: L'Harmattan.

Anders, Gerhard. 2008. "The Normativity of Numbers: World Bank and IMF Conditionality." *Political and Legal Anthropology Review* 31 (2): 187–202.

Atanga Fongue, Roland. 2007. *Contrôle fiscal et protection du contribuable dans un contexte d'ajustement structurel: Le cas du Cameroun.* Paris: L'Harmattan.

Bird, Richard. 2004. "Administrative Dimensions of Tax Reform." *Asia-Pacific Tax Bulletin* 10 (3): 134–50.

Boltanski, Luc, and Eve Chiapello. 2005. *The New Spirit of Capitalism.* London: Verso.

Bruneau, Juliette, and David Abouem. 2004. "Evaluation prospective du Programme National de Gouvernance du Cameroun." United Nations Development Programme, Yaoundé. http://erc.undp.org/evaluationadmin/downloaddocument.html?docid=264.

Chendjou, Léopold. 2004. "Impôts: Le MINFIB harcèle les chefs de centre." *Le Messager*, November 19.

Chaty, Lionel. 1997. *L'administration face au management.* Paris: L'Harmattan.

Clark, David. 1998. "The Modernization of the French Civil Service: Crisis, Change, and Continuity." *Public Administration* 76 (1): 97–115.

Dirsmith, Mark, and Stephen Jablonsky. 1979. "MBO, Political Rationality, and Information Inductance." *Accounting, Organizations and Society* 4 (1–2): 39–52.

Drucker, Peter F. 1954. *The Practice of Management.* New York: Harper.

———. 1976. "What Results Should You Expect? A Users' Guide to MBO." *Public Administration Review* 36 (1): 12–19.

Endong, Hervé. 2011. "Impôts: Près de 60 milliards collectés à Douala en 2010." *La Nouvelle Expression*, February 7.

Evina Obam, Roland. 2005. *L'intégration du pilotage des performances en finances publiques camerounaises.* Master's thesis, École Nationale d'Administration, Strasbourg, France.

Fambon, Samuel. 2006. "Taxation in Developing Countries: Case Study of Cameroon." UNU-WIDER Research Paper 2006/02, World Institute for Development and Economics Research, United Nations University, Helsinki.

Foute, Rousseau-Joël. 2008. "Les explications de Richard Evina Obam: 'Les grandes entreprises bénéficient des gains de productivité.'" *Cameroon Tribune,* October 28.

Gélinier, Octave. 1965. *Morale de l'entreprise et destin de la nation.* Paris: Plon.

———. 1966. *Le secret des structures competitives.* Paris: Hommes et Techniques.

———. 1968. *Direction participative par objectifs.* Paris: Homme et Techniques.

Guyomarch, Alain. 1999. "'Public Service,' 'Public Management,' and the Modernization of French Public Administration." *Public Administration* 77 (1): 171–93.

Hibou, Béatrice. 2006. *La force de l'obéissance: Économie politique de la répression en Tunisie.* Paris: La Découverte.

Holmes, Douglas. 2009. "Economy of Words." *Cultural Anthropology* 24 (3): 381–419.

Hood, Christopher. 1991. "A Public Management for All Seasons?" *Public Administration* 69 (1): 3–19.

Kaldor, Nicholas. 1963. "Will Underdeveloped Countries Learn to Tax?" *Foreign Affairs* 41 (2): 410–19.

Kurunmäki, Liisa, Irvine Lapsley, and Peter Miller. 2011. "Accounting within and beyond the State." *Management Accounting Research* 22 (1): 1–5.

Latour, Bruno. 1996. *Aramis, or the Love of Technology.* Cambridge, MA: Harvard University Press.

Mbodiam, Brice R. 2005. "Des hauts cadres limogés à la suite de contraperformances persistantes." *Mutations,* December 13.

Miller, Peter. 2001. "Governing by Numbers: Why Calculative Practices Matter?" *Social Research* 68 (2): 379–96.

Muñoz, José-María. 2011. "Talking Law in Times of Reform: Paradoxes of Legal Entitlement in Cameroon." *Law and Society Review* 45 (4): 893–921.

Nashashibi, Karim, Abdessatar Ouanes, and Patrick Clawson. 1990. *Les recettes non pétrolières au Cameroun: Analyse et possibilités de réforme.* Washington, DC: International Monetary Fund.

Ngouo, Léon Bertrand. 1997. "Responsibility and Transparency in Governmental Organizations in Cameroon: A Review of Institutional Arrangements." *International Review of Administrative Sciences* 63 (4): 475–92.

———. 2000. "Organizational Development Consulting in the Context of Structural Adjustment in Sub-Saharan Africa: Role and Responsibility of Consultants." *International Review of Administrative Sciences* 66 (1): 105–18.

———. 2008. *Réforme administrative dans les services publics en Afrique: Développement, performance et bonne gouvernance.* Paris: L'Harmattan.

Ossa, René. 2007. *Administrer l'impôt: Les nouveaux enjeux de la fonction de gestion dans les pays en développement.* Yaoundé: Iroko.

Pekassa Ndam, Gérard. 2010. "Les transformations de l'administration fiscale camerounaise." In *L'administration publique camerounaise à l'heure des réformes*, ed. Magloire Ondoa, 29–66. Paris: L'Harmattan.

Porter, Theodore. 1995. *Trust in Numbers.* Princeton, NJ: Princeton University Press.

Radian, Alex. 1980. *Resource Mobilization in Poor Countries: Implementing Tax Policies.* New Brunswick: Transaction.

Raffinot, Marc. 2001. "'Motiver' et 'chicoter': L'économie politique de la pression fiscale en Afrique subsaharienne." *Autrepart* 20 (4): 91–106.

Shore, Chris, Susan Wright, and Davide Pero. 2011. *Policy Worlds: Anthropology and the Analysis of Contemporary Power.* Oxford, U.K.: Berghahn.

Sindjoun, Luc. 1996. "Le champ social camerounais: Désordre inventif, mythes simplificateurs et stabilité hégémonique de l'État." *Politique Africaine* 62: 57–67.

Siwek-Pouydesseau, Jeanne. 1974. "La critique idéologique du management en France." *Revue Française de Science Politique* 24 (5): 966–93.

Strathern, Marilyn. 2000. *Audit Cultures: Anthropological Studies in Accountability, Ethics, and the Academy.* London: Routledge.

———. 2006. "Bullet Proofing: A Tale from the United Kingdom." In *Documents: Artifacts of Modern Knowledge*, ed. Annelise Riles, 181–205. Ann Arbor: University of Michigan Press.

Tamekou, Raoul. 2008. "The National Governance Programme (2006–2010) and the Modernization of the Administration: Cameroon and New Public Management." *International Review of Administrative Sciences* 74 (2): 217–34.

CHAPTER 4

Measuring Performance in the French Customs Administration

Xavier Pascual

The performance measurement system in the French customs administration was introduced as part of a much broader process of modernizing state administrations as a whole by means of an approach based on results, service provided, and performance. Until 2005, customs operations and the activity of all state administrations were essentially determined by budget allocations, with operating appropriations being mechanically carried over and slightly increased each year. The customs administration then used these appropriations to carry out its activity, although this method was not part of a formal strategic framework and no correlation existed between results obtained, objectives established, and resources allocated.

Since 2006 and the effective implementation of the Constitutional Bylaw on Budget Acts (Loi organique relative aux lois de finances, or LOLF), France has introduced more readable and transparent budgets that detail the resources available for the various public policies presented in missions and programs, as well as management by objectives and performance indicators. In developing a results-based culture through the LOLF, the French state seeks to ensure more efficient spending and to enhance the effectiveness of policies for the benefit of all: citizens, public service users, taxpayers, and civil servants.

This chapter describes the performance measurement system established within the French customs administration and its use as a management tool. The first section sets this policy in the general context of a new approach to monitoring the action of all government agencies. The second explains specifically how this performance policy and the various generations of indicators introduced since 2002 have been put in place. Finally, the last section shows how the customs hierarchy deploys the performance tools.

Performance: From National to Local

The general state budget is now presented in terms of major missions (a total of 32 in 2011). These missions identify the major state policies and are divided into programs. Program 302, "Securing and facilitating trade," covers all the activities and appropriations of the General Directorate of Customs and Excise (Direction générale des douanes et droits indirects).

Program 302, Responsibility and Autonomy

Customs is defined as the administration that regulates international trade by means of a dual mission of securing and facilitating such trade. This role involves promoting lawful trade, a contributor to growth, while protecting consumers and the public from fraudulent trade.

The director general of customs is responsible for the program, from defining its strategy and objectives to putting it into practice and reporting on performance to the French parliament.

A focus on objectives is the natural counterpart to broader management autonomy. The LOLF is thus based on striking a balance between the freedom and the responsibility of the manager, who must achieve the prescribed objectives within the respective budget envelope.

Three criteria constituting the three categories of objectives possible are used to assess program performance:

- Socioeconomic objectives, which meet citizens' expectations
- Quality-of-service objectives, which meet users' expectations of the customs administration
- Management efficiency objectives, which meet the expectations of taxpayers, who want the service to be provided at lower cost

Each objective must subsequently be underpinned by the introduction of one or several performance indicators, accompanied by an annual target. The French customs administration thus has five objectives:

- To improve effectiveness in combating fraud and large-scale trafficking
- To increase the speed of customs clearance
- To boost the presence of officers in the field
- To target customs inspections more effectively
- To keep customs management costs under control

To measure progress in meeting these objectives, the French customs administration has defined indicators and has matched them to quantified targets. The French customs performance plan, therefore, now takes the form shown in table 4.1.[1]

Implementation at the Local Level through Several Stages of Management Dialogue

The general framework of Program 302 is put into practice from national to local level by way of three stages of dialogue. The first takes place in the spring between the director general of customs and the Finance

Table 4.1   French Customs Performance Plan

Category of objective	Objective	Performance indicator	Target 2012
Socioeconomic effectiveness (from the citizen's point of view)	To improve effectiveness in combating customs fraud, contraband, and counterfeiting	1. Number of high-value disputed claims	6,200
		2. Amount of seizures of tobacco and cigarettes	€57,500,000
		3. Amount of seizures of narcotics	€340,000,000
		4. Number of investigations into tobacco and cigarettes	13,250
		5. Number of counterfeit articles seized	6,000,000
Quality of service (from the user's point of view)	To increase the speed of customs clearance	6. Time for goods to go through customs	6 minutes, 35 seconds
		7. Overall dematerialization index	81%
Management efficiency (from the taxpayer's point of view)	To boost the presence of officers in the field	8. Rate of availability of monitoring teams	79.4%
	To target inspections more effectively on a risk assessment basis	9. Amount of adjusted duties per investigation	€105,000
		10. Number of significant disputed claims per 10,000 declarations audited	82
	To keep customs management costs under control	11. Intervention rate on customs revenues	0.50%

Source: Le forum de la performance, http://www.performance-publique.budget.gouv.fr/farandole/2012/pap/html/DBGPGMOBJINDPGM302.htm.

Ministry's Budget Directorate, which, since the LOLF came into force, has been responsible for negotiating objectives and monitoring the performance indicators of programs generally, in addition to its traditional missions of ensuring budget programming and expenditure management. The customs administration presents its annual performance plan for the following year with the respective objectives, indicators, and targets, plus all budget and personnel questions. The initial dialogue is thus between the ministry and the director general of customs. Once the plan has been validated, it is included in the government's budget act, which is submitted to parliament in the autumn, when a new stage of dialogue ensues with members of parliament until the act is adopted. In the interval between presentation of the annual performance plan in the spring and its definitive validation by parliament in the autumn, a second round of dialogue takes place between the director general and the interregional customs directors. The LOLF provides for the program leader to make use of operating resources in the form of local managers, who enjoy the same management flexibility at their own level.

Clarification is necessary regarding the level at which management dialogue is applied (that is, the grade at which the performance process is implemented). The French customs administration traditionally consisted of some 40 regional directorates, which were very unequal in size. This structure differed from that of the administrative regions. The customs administration's structure met the specific customs needs of border monitoring and processing of goods entering and leaving national territory at a time when, even within Europe itself, formalities still had to be observed to exchange products between European Community member states.

The notion of an interregional directorate, bringing together several regional directorates, then emerged, though it had no real operational justification. The introduction of the LOLF, local implementation of the performance system, and granting of greater budget autonomy in return for making local decision makers accountable for performance system objectives meant the French customs administration had to decide the level at which the system was to be implemented. The customs administration had decided from the outset that implementation would be through interregional directorates at the local level. The aim was to make this new process of autonomy and accountability meaningful by using a framework that was sufficiently broad to allow the local manager to have a critical mass of appropriations and sufficiently powerful policy instruments for taking action. The regional directorate level was retained as a mere local operational framework for the interregional director's use in implementing the respective strategy.

The 11 territorial interregional directors (plus the directors of the overseas territories and the heads of four national services: intelligence and investigations, recruitment and vocational training, customs information technology center, and foreign trade statistics) are therefore the direct and only intermediaries of the director general of the French customs administration. The 11 interregional directorates (strategic level for the performance process and management dialogue) and the 40 regional directorates (operational level) are shown on map 4.1.

The interregional directors therefore have fresh room for maneuver in allocating their appropriations, but they also set the objectives and targets to be met, which are local versions of national objectives and targets. A chain of responsibility and management dialogue has therefore been put

Map 4.1   French Interregional Customs Directorates

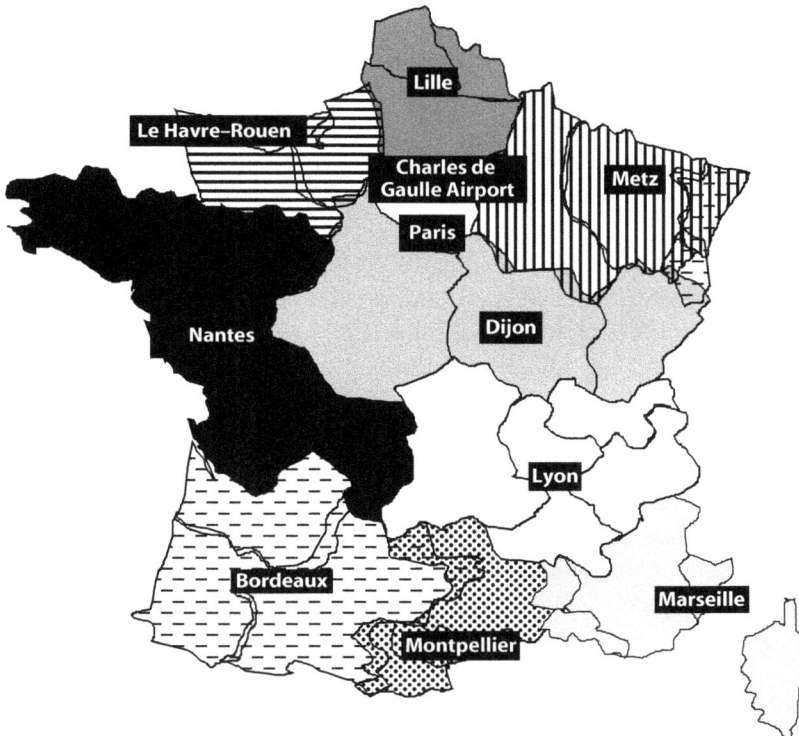

Source: French customs administration, 2011 data.

in place to ensure that the customs administration is governed by performance and that management is further devolved.

The finalizing of the national framework arising out of the performance meeting marks the opening of management dialogue between the director general and the interregional directors on issues connected to the budget, personnel, and performance. In June, the director general sends the interregional directors a single project outline. This reference document should provide them with guidance in drawing up their budget and local performance plan.

In terms of performance, the outline leads to the proposal of targets for each interregional director. In sectors where the indicator is quantitative (for example, amount of narcotics seized), the sum of the targets apportioned among the interregional directorates corresponds to the national target. The interregional directors may accept or reject the targets proposed.

At the end of August, the interregional directors forward their draft budget and performance plan to the General Directorate of Customs and Excise. This document is examined by each subdirectorate of the General Directorate, and points of disagreement on targets or appropriations are discussed bilaterally in September.

In October, each interregional director attends a management meeting at the General Directorate of Customs and Excise. The meeting is chaired by the deputy director general and is attended by representatives of all subdirectorates. This half-day exercise gives each director the opportunity to address not only issues relating to performance, the budget, and personnel, but also all current issues and activity concerns in his or her area. The meeting closes with the approval of the draft budget and performance plan and the joint determination of objectives ascribed to the director for the following year.

During implementation of the performance plan, a third stage of dialogue is held at the local level. Meetings are organized interregionally to monitor the development of results, to determine whether the target can actually be met, and to consider corrective measures if it cannot. Management dialogue and performance monitoring should thus give rise to collective and continuous work throughout the year.

A Process in the French Customs Administration that Broadly Exceeds the Exclusive Framework of the Budget Act

The performance process, initially formalized through annual performance plans alone, has developed in three other forms and also applies to other exercises. The first form is the *multiannual performance contract*. The formal framework of the annual performance plan has the advantage of being highly structured, readable, and succinct. It is therefore a suitable format in which to demonstrate to parliament the social usefulness of the customs administration. Internally, when addressing customs officers, it may be seen as too limited or restrictive, because it does not cover all areas of intervention.

What is more, the purely annual perspective of performance plans may appear too limited when a medium-term strategy and objectives have to be formulated for the customs administration that all officers will endorse. The French customs administration thus opted for a multiannual performance contract, a more complete document geared essentially toward customs officers.

Preparation of the multiannual performance contract is discussed not only within the General Directorate of Customs and Excise, but also in workshops with customs officers and heads of service to take more areas of customs intervention into account, to determine a medium-term strategy for each of them, and to introduce appropriate performance indicators. This process has led to the identification of four commitments:

- Customs, the administration of services
- Customs, the administration of protection
- Customs, a modern tax administration
- Customs, a staff-centered administration

Eight indicators have been identified for each commitment—that is, a total of 32 indicators (some of which also appear in the annual performance plan). These indicators are as often as possible defined in cooperation with officers or heads of service who perform the activity themselves.

The second form of the performance process is *employee participation*. Like many public administrations, the French customs administration has introduced a collective employee participation scheme. Among the indicators in the multiannual performance contract, 12 have been highlighted, because they are considered to be the most representative of customs administration action.

The number of targets met determines the amount of the employee participation bonus. The scheme is national and collective, which means that, for a given year, all customs officers, irrespective of service and grade, receive the same amount of bonus. The bonus is relatively modest, because the maximum that can be received for one year (€150) corresponds to about 10 percent of the monthly salary of the lowest-grade customs officer at the beginning of his or her career.

The third form of the performance policy is the *exemplary administration plan*. The performance measurement system is now so widespread that it goes beyond the framework of exercising customs activity alone and is applied in much broader areas. Although the following example is undeniably anecdotal, it is nevertheless revealing. Since 2010, an interministerial scheme has prompted all government agencies, including customs, to operate on a sustainable development basis. Accordingly, the Ministry of the Environment has defined a list of 14 indicators that includes, for example, the number of reams of paper used per officer per year, the number of rooms equipped with video-conferencing facilities, the energy expenses of buildings, or the percentage of vehicles purchased that comply with the standard of 120 grams of carbon dioxide per kilometer. At the beginning of the year, all administrations have to pay a contribution into an interministerial fund, and at the end of the year, this sum is shared only among administrations that have met at least 11 of the 14 targets.

The performance process now applies to many aspects of public management, inside and outside customs. However, it is not used for transparency or corruption issues, because these issues are not seen as relevant in France.

From Measurement of Activity to Measurement of Performance: The Difficulty of Producing Indicators

As demonstrated in the previous section, the French customs administration has established its performance measurement process in several stages. Each exercise gives rise to the introduction of performance indicators to measure the results and progress made.

The choice or production of an indicator is determined by several principles that have been widely documented in the literature on performance. Accordingly, a good indicator should meet the following criteria:

- It should be relevant—that is, capable of measuring the desired effect or trend.
- It should be useful and meaningful—that is, the result provided should be interpretable and should provide the reader with clarification.
- It should be robust—that is, its scope should be clearly defined and its component elements should be objective and quantifiable.

- It should be reliable and verifiable—that is, the mathematic operations leading to the result should be clear and reproducible so that reliability is beyond doubt.

In addition to these theoretical conditions, the French customs administration has gradually developed its own specific body of theory on indicators on an empirical basis, formulating several general principles on the nature and use of indicators and the aspects they should measure.

Formulation of a Body of Theory on the Use of Indicators

Practice has led the French customs administration to highlight four supplementary principles governing the creation, distribution, and definition of the scope of indicators. First, indicators must be automated. The establishment of an indicator arises out of a dual process: (a) what the indicator is considered relevant to measure, and (b) what is technically possible to calculate automatically from the existing information system.

The French customs administration starts from the premise that it now has a plethora of computer applications and teleservices whose statistics retrieval capabilities are often misunderstood and underused. Full advantage must therefore be taken of information system capabilities, and recourse to manual statistics or surveys of services must be avoided. Hence, staff members should no longer be asked to fill in management charts or statistical tables on their activity, because such a task represents a significant workload and the data entered often cannot be verified. Asking them to work on national computer applications while completing statistical tables on paper at the same time is therefore pointless and ineffective.

Thus, when a customs officer performs a particular operation on a computer application while carrying out an activity (for example, subjecting a customs declaration to inspection or drawing up a disputed claim document), an indicator is automatically raised. In general, when the information system does not allow the forwarding of information and automated calculations, a choice is made not to create an indicator rather than create an indicator that would entail the use of manual operations.

In the case of qualitative indicators—for example, regarding quality of service—surveys are not done by customs, but by the Finance Ministry. Every six months, a polling organization surveys companies and the public, asking them their opinion of the customs administration, the revenue administration, and so on. Some of the answers to the questions about customs are used as quality indicators.

Second, the rules for calculating indicators are published and periodically discussed with the interested parties. All indicators are documented; they are covered in a one- or two-page file that specifies their usefulness, method of calculation, and scope. These files are available online on the customs intranet and can be consulted by all officers.

The Management Control Unit (Cellule de contrôle de gestion, or CCG) also regularly brings together officers and heads of service who carry out activities covered by a particular indicator to reflect jointly on the relevance of that indicator (some may have become insignificant or pointless), desired developments in scope (to take new products or flows into account), creation of new indicators intended to reflect the new strategy in the sector of activity, and so on.

Third, the results of indicators can be seen at all hierarchical levels. The dissemination of indicator results has long been regarded as a sensitive issue. Regional decision makers initially were very reluctant to see the results of their indicators passed on, whether within their service to officers or among peers. Gradually, however, a more transparent approach has developed as the performance process has become increasingly accepted, the objectives pursued have become familiar and shared, and the indicators themselves have been recognized as reliable and significant. On the one hand, regional decision makers wanted to be able to compare themselves with their colleagues; on the other hand, they felt that transparency among all levels of the hierarchical chain, including officers in the field, was a means of ensuring the greatest possible support for the approach.

Finally, the indicators are applied to customs *services*, never to customs officers individually. The strategy and objectives defined are those of the French customs administration in general, and all services participate in implementing them. Targets and performance measurement are developed at interregional director level or lower grades, however, though never by customs officers themselves.

In the early years of implementing performance measurement, interregional directors often set targets at service and team levels. The risk arose, however, that officers would focus too much on their individual figures and results to the detriment of collective results and the customs service as a whole.

Individual interests may not be compatible with the collective interest. If an individual's only focus is a figure, a risk arises that individuals may work only toward achieving that figure. They may neglect work in cooperation with colleagues and the other services, and they may lose the overall vision of the medium- and long-term strategy and objectives. The activity, working methods, and action plan implementation must be given pride of place to improve results, effectiveness, and efficiency, whereas indicators must be left in the background: they are measured automatically and, at the end of the period, will reflect the progress made.

Three Generations of Indicators for More Qualitative Performance Measurement

The purpose of indicators used to underpin a performance process must be to reflect not the activity of the customs service but its results and performance in particular—that is, the improvement in its effectiveness and efficiency in carrying out its missions. Table 4.2 highlights these different notions and gives an example of an indicator corresponding to them.

Indicators were introduced into the French customs administration gradually, and generations of different types of indicators can be distinguished. The first generation measured activity and results. These indicators still exist and are still used, but because they were the first to be produced, they correspond to measurements that were already carried out before the performance approach was introduced in 2003.

This first generation was purely quantitative; that is, it measured only activity or results. This type of measurement was a traditional fixture in the French customs administration, as it was in most customs services in the world. It is therefore not a result of the introduction of the performance approach but has been assimilated into it.

An example of activity indicators is the number of inspections carried out. Such an indicator may be useful to verify the presence of officers in the field and their mobilization, but increasing the number of inspections is not an objective in itself. Public expectations of the customs administration are not that it should carry out inspections, but that it should get results in combating large-scale trafficking.

It is therefore often more useful to establish results indicators that focus on seizures of narcotics, smuggled tobacco and cigarettes, counterfeit

Table 4.2   Sample Indicator

Activity ➜	Result ➜	Effectiveness ➜	Efficiency
Number of inspections carried out	Number of disputed claims brought or quantities seized	Percentage of inspections that have led to a disputed claim	Costs incurred in bringing a disputed claim

Source: World Bank.

goods, weapons, or species protected by the Convention on International Trade in Endangered Species of Wild Fauna and Flora (CITES, known as the Washington Convention). These indicators relate to core customs activities and bear witness to the mobilization of services in combating fraud and the effectiveness of inspections.

Nevertheless, assessing the performance of a particular service on the basis of these indicators is difficult. The customs service does not control the supply of illicit products that arrive on the market. The seizure of smaller quantities may mean that the service is less effective, but it may also indicate that customs activity has had a dissuasive effect and that fewer illicit products overall are present in national territory. The insufficiency of this measurement of results soon became apparent.

Since 2005, a second generation of indicators has been used to take the notion of effectiveness and the qualitative dimension into account. As stated previously, what the public really expects of the customs service is not that it should carry out inspections, but that it should get results in combating large-scale trafficking. Within the customs administration, however, the director's expectations go further: not only are quantitative results wanted, but in a context of limited resources, the director wants an increasing proportion of inspections to lead to disputed claims and the disputed claims brought to be significant.

A fundamental indicator in French Customs offices is *the effectiveness of customs declaration controls* (see indicator 10 in table 4.1). It measures the proportion of customs declarations inspected or audited in the customs clearance system that give rise to significant disputed claims. The effectiveness of the targeting of customs declarations must therefore be improved through a risk analysis mechanism. In France, this task is carried out by specialized services operating at national and regional levels; in each customs office, a supervisory officer is responsible for implementing and monitoring the effectiveness of the risk analysis mechanisms. Because the indicator is a ratio between the number of declarations controlled and the number of significant disputed claims brought, the result will be improved mainly by reducing the number of declarations controlled. The supervisor's role is therefore to identify inspections that never give rise to disputed claims.

This indicator, therefore, means controlling less but controlling better. Risk analysis thus ensures better targeting of declarations to be audited but should also allow more serious frauds to be detected and significant disputed claims to be brought.

The French customs administration thus calls for its services to reduce the number of inspections and to ensure that an increasing proportion of such inspections gives rise to disputed claims, as well as to ensure that the disputed claims brought are as significant as possible. The notion of high-value disputed claims—that is, significant disputed claims—was therefore created and given an indicator.

Ceilings have been defined for each type of disputed claim (narcotics, tobacco, counterfeiting, weapons, Washington Convention) above which a claim is classified as high value (that is, significant), and the *number of high-value disputed claims* indicator is regarded as a priority within the customs administration (see indicator 1 in table 4.1).

The high-value threshold for each type of disputed claim is determined as follows. For values of narcotics seized, for example, all the narcotics claims brought over the past three years are ranked in decreasing order (from the highest to the lowest value); the first 15 percent of the claims on this list are considered; the lowest value of the top 15 percent is taken, and the value of the narcotics seized is noted. This amount thus becomes the threshold beyond which a disputed claim is classified as high value in the future.

This exercise is repeated for each type of disputed claim, thus producing a threshold in each area that enables a claim to be classified as high value or not. An indicator then compiles the number of high-value disputed claims brought for each service.

Another example of an indicator that seeks to take into account a more qualitative dimension of the work of services records *disputed claims brought in cooperation* among several services. A well-known unintended effect of indicators is that officers or services may be encouraged only to seek immediate results and to behave individualistically to raise their own indicators. Furthermore, most officers themselves fear such an effect. To offset this effect, as explained previously, an indicator applies to a service rather than to an individual officer. All officers in the service must therefore contribute to achieving the targets set.

The same difficulty, however, may then arise at the level of the various services. One service might bring a low-value disputed claim that would raise its indicators rather than passing the information on to another service, which would be in a position to bring a higher-value disputed claim, thereby raising the latter's indicators but not the former's.

The French customs administration believes that a condition for success in combating fraud, in particular, is the exchange of information between services and work on investigations and actions carried out in cooperation by several services. It has therefore opted to incorporate this dimension of cooperation between services and to enhance it by means of the system of indicators. This approach operates in two ways: by means of a *disputed claims brought in cooperation* indicator and by means of disputed claims awards rules.

In the first case, an indicator related to the number of claims brought in cooperation is created. When several services are involved in a disputed claim, one takes the lead (its *quantities of narcotics seized* indicator is raised), while the others take part by way of cooperation (their *number of disputed claims in cooperation* indicator is raised). The *quantities of narcotics* indicator is therefore raised only once and is attributed to a service, but when the number of disputed claims brought by a particular service is studied, the number in which it has been involved only in cooperation is added to the number it has brought. This measurement involves adding together the result of two indicators that operate separately. No indicator related to a number of claims combines those brought individually and those brought in cooperation; otherwise the same claims would be recorded several times, and the sum of the disputed claims per service would not correspond to the national result.

In the second case, the customs administration chooses to promote an indicator internally, and local heads of service are asked to ensure that they present it and make it understandable to the services. The General Directorate of Customs and Excise has also adopted certain disputed claims award rules that seek to further encourage the exchange of information and collaborative work. Thus, if a service located in a port or airport discovers narcotics in a freight shipment, it may pass on the information to another service capable of bringing a higher-value disputed claim (for example, because the address of the final destination of the goods is a warehouse that may contain further quantities). The first service therefore makes the other service aware of the shipment, and in return, the latter enters the destination warehouse and draws up the legal paperwork for the quantities discovered initially and the additional quantities that may be discovered in the destination warehouse.

In such a case, the rule would mechanically increase the *quantity of goods seized* indicator of the second service that seizes the goods and increase the *disputed claims brought in cooperation* indicator of the first service. However, in a determined effort to promote cooperation between services, the General Directorate of Customs and Excise has structured the system so that it is the first service—the one that made the initial discovery but opted to cooperate—whose *quantities of goods seized* indicator is raised, whereas the second service is credited with the *disputed claims brought in cooperation* indicator. This allocation shows the priority given to collaborative work and the exchange of information rather than to seizure.

Since 2007 and the introduction of a new automated customs clearance system, a third generation of indicators has been designed to take account of the effect of customs administration activity on the economy and on society. This type of indicator corresponds to a more comprehensive and holistic approach by measuring not an action carried out by the customs administration itself but the impact of that service's action on its environment in relation to the objectives it has set itself.

This measurement corresponds, for example, to estimations of a "tax gap" or "contraband gap." In this case, the aim is to measure not the amount of taxes collected but the gap between the amount of taxes actually collected and the amount of taxes that should have been collected. Some specific studies are being carried out, but they are too complex, occasional, and specific to lead to the creation of a perennial indicator.

This indicator also corresponds to "time-release studies," which measure port turnaround times, models of which are used by international organizations. In France, the customs administration does not conduct this type of study, but in clearing goods, an indicator of *average time for goods to go through customs* indicator has been introduced to meet the objective of increasing customs clearance speed. This indicator measures the average time between the moment an importer validates a customs declaration in the customs clearance system and the moment the customs administration gives the importer a definitive status for its goods: "customs clearance accepted" or "customs clearance refused." Given that the date and time of validation of the declaration and the award of status are recorded in the customs clearance system, calculating the average processing period is easy. In 2010, the result of this indicator was 6 minutes and 19 seconds, compared with 5 minutes and 57 seconds in 2011.

This indicator is clearly meaningless in terms of a single import operation carried out by a single operator: no goods were cleared through customs in 6 minutes and 19 seconds in 2010 or in 5 minutes and 57 seconds in 2011, and no operator will be delighted that its goods were released 22 seconds earlier in 2011 than in 2010. For the customs service, however, this indicator is meaningful at a global level. A fall in the average turnaround time indicates the following possibilities:

- A greater proportion of customs declarations have passed through the green channel (no control) with a turnaround time of several seconds (that is, the technical time for receiving an answer), and a lower proportion of declarations have gone through the red channel (subject to control) because risk analysis centers and targeting units have introduced more effective selection criteria and have removed criteria that would generate inspections without ever generating disputed claims.

- A greater number of mandatory supporting documents have been presented in electronic form, and the system has been able to review them automatically: declarations that used to be inspected by the system to verify the presence and validity of health or veterinary documents no longer go through because this inspection is automated (single window approach).

- When goods are under customs control, the customs officer is in a position to decide more quickly whether they comply thanks to various instruments or tools: posting on the customs administration intranet of regulations and data sheets indicating how to distinguish authentic goods from counterfeit goods, prior delivery of binding tariff information to the operator, and so on.

- The availability and performance of customs clearance computer applications is improving.

Therefore the principal characteristic and advantage of this indicator is as an indicator of impact, the result of which reflects not the effect of a single action but the effect of a range of actions, all of which the customs administration is responsible for. It is therefore a strategic indicator that is very significant for all customs administration actions and efforts. Nevertheless, it is not a client-oriented indicator, and it is used only for internal management.

Performance-Managed Services

From a simple budgetary constraint, performance has gradually come to the fore as a management tool in the French customs administration.

The Management Control Unit, an Independent Structure Devoted to the Rigorous Production of Figures

Within the French General Directorate of Customs and Excise, the CCG (*Cellule de Contrôle de gestion* [Management Control Unit]) is responsible for calculating and publishing the results of most indicators. Set up in 2003, the CCG is currently staffed by eight officers and forms a specific structure within the General Directorate, which is, in turn, made up of six large subdirectorates dealing with the following areas: organization of services and human resources, budget and equipment, information system, legal and political aspects of controls, international trade, and taxation. When the CCG was set up, several options were considered for its location:

- Within the subdirectorate responsible for organizing services and monitoring activity
- Within the subdirectorate responsible for allocating budget resources
- As an autonomous service not forming part of any subdirectorate but attached directly to the director general

The last option was selected. The CCG is therefore positioned at a high level (its head is a member of the governing board of the French customs administration), and its independence allows it to take a cross-cutting approach and to have a global vision of matters.

The legitimacy and credibility of the CCG were built up gradually and have now reached a satisfactory level. It has thus become the General Directorate of Custom and Excise's "numbers bureau": that is, it is responsible for calculating or at least validating the figures recorded in the activity report of the French customs administration. Thus, the Information and Communication Office of the customs administration, which publishes many files and documents for the press or the general public, always has the figures it includes in its publications approved by the CCG.

Early January is therefore a particularly sensitive time for the CCG: at that time, the results of all performance indicators are compiled and made more reliable in preparation for drafting the customs administration's official activity report for the preceding year. This report is traditionally presented during the final week of January by the budget minister, who oversees the customs service, at a press conference that is always well attended. It is therefore crucial for the figures given out at this time to be reliable and justifiable, because they will then be deemed definitive.[2] The figure announced at the press conference is thus the official figure, which is not subject to change.

Although this method seems clear, it is, in fact, a severe constraint for the customs service: at the press conference, for example, the customs administration announces the figure for the quantity of narcotics seized in the preceding year. In technical terms, it is the result of the *quantities of narcotics seized* indicator, which is automated, and the management rule is that a file only counts toward the indicator when it is definitively closed by a regional director's decision on the action to be taken (for example, transaction with or without penalties, legal proceedings). Several days, if not weeks, therefore have to elapse between the discovery of a product suspected of being a narcotic, the tests allowing its nature to be verified, the drafting of the procedural documents, the creation of the disputed claim file in the information system, and the various stages of hierarchical validation of the file up to a final statement that triggers an increase in the indicator.

For a discovery of narcotics made at the end of December 2011, there is thus a substantial risk that the process will not be entirely concluded by January 16, 2012, the date "the meters shut down" for calculating the official figure for 2011. Only one official figure exists for drug seizures in 2011—the one announced in January by the minister at a press conference—and it is a definitive figure that cannot be changed. Quantities of narcotics seized at the end of December but for which the file has not been validated before January 16 will not be included either in the 2011 report or in the 2012 report (since it will no longer be the same reference year). The file is therefore "lost" in terms of performance measurement.

This internal rule is particularly rigorous but forms the basis of the credibility of a process for generating statistics for the French customs administration. The consequence is therefore that all French customs services devote the end of the year and the beginning of the following year to completing and increasing the reliability of all files that can raise their performance indicators.

The CCG and the Production of Studies on the Efficiency of Services
The CCG positions itself as a statistics service for the French customs administration—a guarantor of the quality of the data produced—but it also sees its role as that of an expert at the service of the director general, the director general's activity subdirectorates, and the interregional directors. The CCG thus compares either different services within the same regional directorate or similar services in different regions of France (for example, port or airport services).

In addition to the results of performance indicators, data are collected on the costs of services (payroll costs, cost of building leases, cost of vehicles, and the like). Such data are cross-referenced to produce studies and graphs that show the relationship between the results of services in terms of combating fraud and their cost.

Costs are measured in various stages:

- *Stage 1.* Direct costs, corresponding to the appropriations used, are measured.

- *Stage 2.* Some of these stage 1 costs must be standardized. This step involves reprocessing the direct cost to neutralize certain parameters so that a comparison can be drawn. For example, regions in the south of France are more attractive than those in the north, and civil service transfer and assignment rules mean that customs officers secure a post in the south of France at a more advanced age. Accordingly, the average age of customs officers and, therefore, the personnel costs of director-ates in the south of France are much greater than they are in director-ates in the north of France. Personnel cost standardization therefore involves reducing personnel expenditure to an average cost per officer, though taking grade into account.

- *Stage 3.* Indirect costs are taken into account; that is, part of the support costs (for example, supervision and vocational training costs) is added.

- *Stage 4.* The full standard cost, or *global cost*, is calculated. That is, the direct costs, some standardized, are increased by a proportion of the cost of support actions.

This method of calculating costs is then used to measure the efficiency of services. Here again, as for measuring results and effectiveness, the CCG proposes what to measure to the heads of the General Directorate's activity subdirectorates and the interregional directors, who are in a posi-tion to give an opinion on the usefulness, relevance, and possible signifi-cance to be attributed to a particular measurement.

Two examples of a customs service comparative efficiency measure-ment follow.

Example 1. For customs services that carry out controls on roads, motor-ways, ports, and airports (excluding customs clearance activity), the

General Directorate of Customs and Excise produces a graph for each interregion that highlights the full standard cost of each service on the one hand and its results in combating fraud on the other. In consultation with the interregional directors, the General Directorate has decided to highlight the notion of results in combating fraud by recording, as previously explained, the number of high-value disputed claims brought, whether by this service alone or in cooperation with another service. Each service is then placed on the graph according to its results, thus showing the relative efficiency of each service within an interregion. Figure 4.1 is an example of such a graph. The farther to the bottom right a service is placed, the more it achieves results without costing very much, and thus the more efficient it is considered. Such graphs are also produced for comparable services in several different interregions (for example, to compare customs services located in border areas).

Example 2. The General Directorate of Customs and Excise has tried another approach for customs offices that process customs declarations. This approach involves cross-referencing, on the one hand, the efficiency of offices, as expressed by the number of customs declarations processed by each officer, and on the other hand, their effectiveness, as expressed by the number of high-value disputed claims brought per 100 customs

Figure 4.1   Efficiency of Monitoring Teams

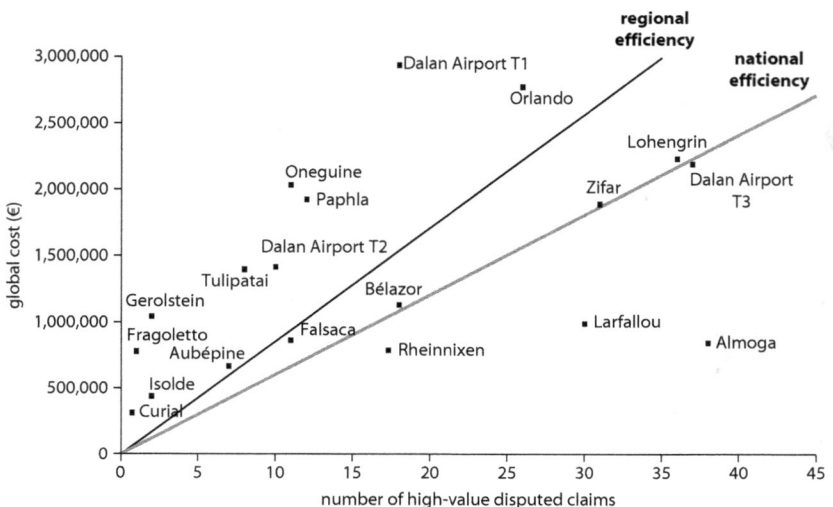

Source: French customs administration, 2011 data.

Figure 4.2   Effectiveness and Efficiency of Customs Offices

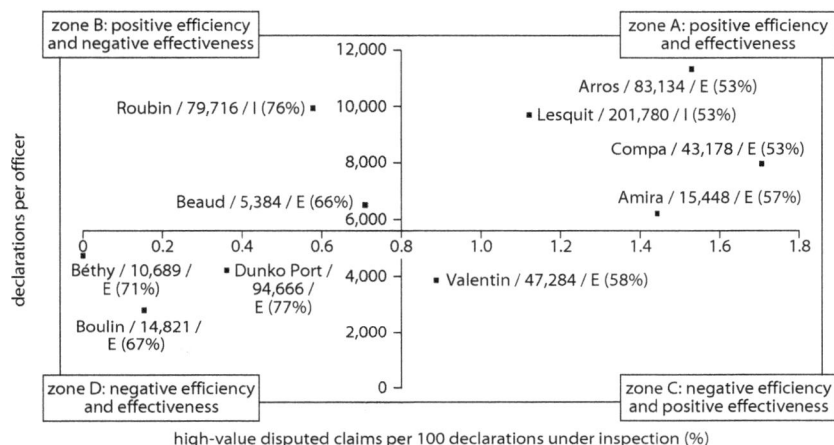

Source: French customs administration, 2011 data.

declarations classified as "subject to control" in the customs clearance application (indicator of the effectiveness of the inspection of declarations, as previously described).

Figure 4.2 is an example of this type of graph. Here again, the method for drawing up these graphs was proposed by the General Directorate of Customs and Excise but discussed and accepted by the interregional directors. As stated previously, local directors need to accept the criteria on which the performance of their services is to be assessed.

These graphs have led to the highlighting of offices in zone A that combine a significant number of declarations processed per officer and the high effectiveness of their targeting with a view to a control; of offices in zones B and C that meet only one criterion; and of offices in zone D that do not meet any. An examination of these results also allows conclusions to be drawn concerning the optimum size of customs offices. Moreover, it has often been noted that significant activity motivates officers and improves the effectiveness of their work.

Conclusion

Performance measurement is now recognized as an element of management dialogue and a tool for managing services. Several conclusions can be drawn.

Indicators Support Management Dialogue

Even if many areas remain to be investigated and much room remains for improvement in exploiting the figures produced, the French customs administration has undoubtedly reached a relatively stable situation, with a coherent range of reliable and consolidated indicators and well-defined and accepted exercises for using them. Performance measurement has become a significant element of management dialogue between central and regional levels and is considered to be essential at a time of budgetary constraints and staff cuts.

Management dialogue is now regarded as rich and responsible, and conferences on the theme give rise to useful exchanges of views. The interregional directors often prepare for the debates that arise in these conferences well in advance, and they fully accept their role as local budget and performance managers. Stakeholders as a whole have gained a particular maturity in their understanding and intelligent use of the results of indicators, of the work on efficiency, and of performance measurement more globally.

The graphs (see figures 4.1 and 4.2), like indicators in general, should be used in the manner clearly intended. They present a record or inventory of the situation of a particular service compared to its objectives. The aim of indicators and graphs of this type is to establish a record that is based on a universally accepted methodology and databases.

Indicators Make it Possible to Clarify Objectives but Do Not State How to Achieve Them

Indicators are management tools that serve the interests of managers, but they are not instruments for change per se. The instruments for change are measurements defined by the activities themselves. The creation of an indicator does not in itself allow a situation to be improved. The indicator may at best have a mobilizing effect, because officers will perceive the activity measured to be strategic. Thus, the indicator will allow progress made to be measured, but it does not determine what action should be taken to achieve the progress sought. The latter aspect, which is essential, is the responsibility of the activities and should involve activity measurements (new intervention methods, service reorganization, analysis development, and so on).

Indicators Indicate, but They Do Not Make Decisions

The objective record that indicators allow to be drawn up serves as the basis for discussion to

- Identify the services that have developed good practices.
- Pool the use of such good practices.
- Help management to allocate personnel, budget resources, and equipment.

Management control has undoubtedly come to the fore in a context of budgetary constraint and is therefore often associated with restructuring. Management control is accepted, however, if the reforms decided concern customs activities and arise out of such activities. Efficiency graphs such as those presented in figures 4.1 and 4.2 thus make it possible to determine the services that contribute least to achieving customs service results and to global performance. However, no automatic link exists between measuring a situation and making decisions.

Once again, the aim of indicators is to provide decision makers (the director general, regional directors) with objective data on the performance of a service, but such data are just one of the parameters managers take into account before making decisions. Political, social, and environmental considerations are also examined before any decision is made.

Indicators should be used only for what they are capable of doing well and only when they have been well chosen and defined. They provide a snapshot of the state of progress or implementation of a project or strategy, and they enable the progress made or difficulties encountered to be assessed and, therefore, allow lessons to be learned.

The CCG bases its legitimacy on the quality of its expertise. The figures it produces should provide a snapshot of a situation that is as objective as possible, but they should also help in analyzing the components of the results. Merely measuring the annual increase in results is insufficient; one must also be able to show why and how that increase is brought about. Performance figures are therefore tools at the service of managers, who guide the action of services and lead and support change.

Notes

1. This table can be consulted online at http://www.performance-publique. budget.gouv.fr/farandole/2012/pap/html/DBGPGMOBJINDPGM302.htm. This site provides access to all annual performance plans for all budget programs.

2. By way of example, the 2011 report was presented by the minister on January 26, 2012, and it gave rise to the publication of final figures (General Directorate of Customs and Excise 2012).

Reference

General Directorate of Customs and Excise. 2012. "Douane: Le défi de la regulation des échanges." General Directorate of Customs and Excise, Montreuil, France. http://www.douane.budget.gouv.fr/data/file/7369.pdf.

CHAPTER 5

Inspecting Less to Inspect Better

The Use of Data Mining for Risk Management by Customs Administrations

Anne-Marie Geourjon, Bertrand Laporte, Ousmane Coundoul, and Massène Gadiaga

Under the revised Kyoto Convention on the simplification and harmonization of customs procedures, the World Customs Organization recommends that intrusive customs inspections be limited (WCO 2003). This proposal has also been discussed in the context of World Trade Organization trade facilitation negotiations.[1] Therefore, despite the temptation to ramp up systematic inspections in light of the events of September 11, 2001, the most modern customs administrations have continued to rely on risk analysis as the only effective means for both facilitating trade and securing their own operations, given the important growth in trade volume in recent years (Harrison and Holloway 2007).

Customs administrations of developing countries also should have a structured approach to risk analysis when determining how to process a particular trade transaction (Walsh 2003; Widdowson 2005). These countries are simultaneously confronted by growth in trade flows and demands of private operators as well as by pressures placed on them by governments to mobilize revenues. However, they have been slow to move in this direction and to implement the latest risk analysis and risk management techniques (Geourjon and Laporte 2005; Geourjon, Rota Graziosi, and Laporte 2010; Hintsa and others 2011).

The information systems used by customs administrations in developing countries screen declarations by defining and applying iterative selection rules using dual, largely qualitative criteria and random targeting. The traditional selection methods used in the electronic customs clearance systems of these countries remain very dependent on human judgment, which represents a major shortcoming, given moral hazard. These systems are also static and rigid because the rules governing them are seldom updated, allowing fraudsters to modify their behavior to avoid detection.

Private inspection companies working in developing countries offer risk analysis services to customs administrations as part of their contracts with governments to carry out preshipment and destination inspection and scanning services. The systems these companies offer are standardized and are based on their own data. Customs administrations, therefore, have difficulty adapting the companies' data to their purposes and, in practice, seldom use the data in the selection process for their inspections, which essentially continue to be based on their own traditional methods. The difficulty arises because the risk analysis services offered by the private inspection companies and the import verification programs that they were contracted to provide have two conflicting objectives. The aim of risk analysis services is to modernize administration procedures, which implies a partnership between customs and the private company, whereas in import verification, the effectiveness of the double-checking system relies on customs and the private company being independent of one another to avoid any hint of collusion. The two services—inspection and risk analysis—are therefore incompatible in the same contract. Moreover, the companies that offer the latter base this service purely on the data collected during the course of their own inspections (Dequiedt, Geourjon, and Rota Graziosi 2009, 2012).

In the majority of developing countries, particularly in Sub-Saharan Africa, customs administrations continue to carry out intrusive inspections of large numbers of containers, resulting in the proportion of detected incidences of fraud generally being less than 3 percent (as is the case in Benin, Burkina Faso, Côte d'Ivoire, Mali, and Senegal, for instance). Customs administrations therefore need to develop their own risk analysis and management systems that will be modern, effective, and based on customs data so that they can inspect fewer containers but more effectively. The idea is to adapt the risk analysis methods used in many other sectors, such as banking, insurance, and security, to the context of customs.

In practice, applying risk analysis in every sector and in every organization would require a specific approach in each case (Gates 2006).

This chapter aims to show that data mining and relatively simple statistical scoring methods can allow customs administrations in developing countries to assess risk and hence to effectively limit inspections. The chapter also shows that developing these techniques will contribute to the modernization of customs administrations. Following a description of some of these techniques, the chapter outlines how the techniques have been implemented in West Africa and assesses their use in Senegal. It then analyzes the effects of those techniques on the modernization process.

Statistical Scoring Techniques for Measuring Risk: An Innovative Tool for Customs

The goal of reform is to design a system that will assist customs administrations in effectively deciding which transactions to inspect. Although already in use in many other sectors, statistical scoring techniques are seldom used by customs administrations in developing countries. However, the advantages of the techniques are far greater than simply carrying out valuation or tariff classification controls. A recent study by Grigoriou (2012) shows the advantages of statistical scoring for carrying out inspections with a view to enforcing technical, sanitary, and phytosanitary regulations.

Customs Information Systems: Information Flows That Need to Be Organized

All risk analysis depends on information, which needs to be available and processed correctly. The main obstacle to developing systems based on data mining is the absence of reliable data on detected incidences of fraud. This lack of data may have one of two causes: (a) weaknesses among customs administrations in litigating offenses and (b) poor traceability of data relating to that litigation (customs violation reporting). Nonetheless, significant information flows concerning customs fraud are available and should be processed to analyze overall risk and to manage it. Figure 5.1 distinguishes between data on confirmed fraud and data on suspected fraud.

Use of risk analysis and management to assign declarations to the various inspection channels depends mainly on use of existing historical data on detected incidents of fraud over a given period. The results obtained

Figure 5.1   Information Flows on Customs Fraud Theoretically Available to Customs Administrations

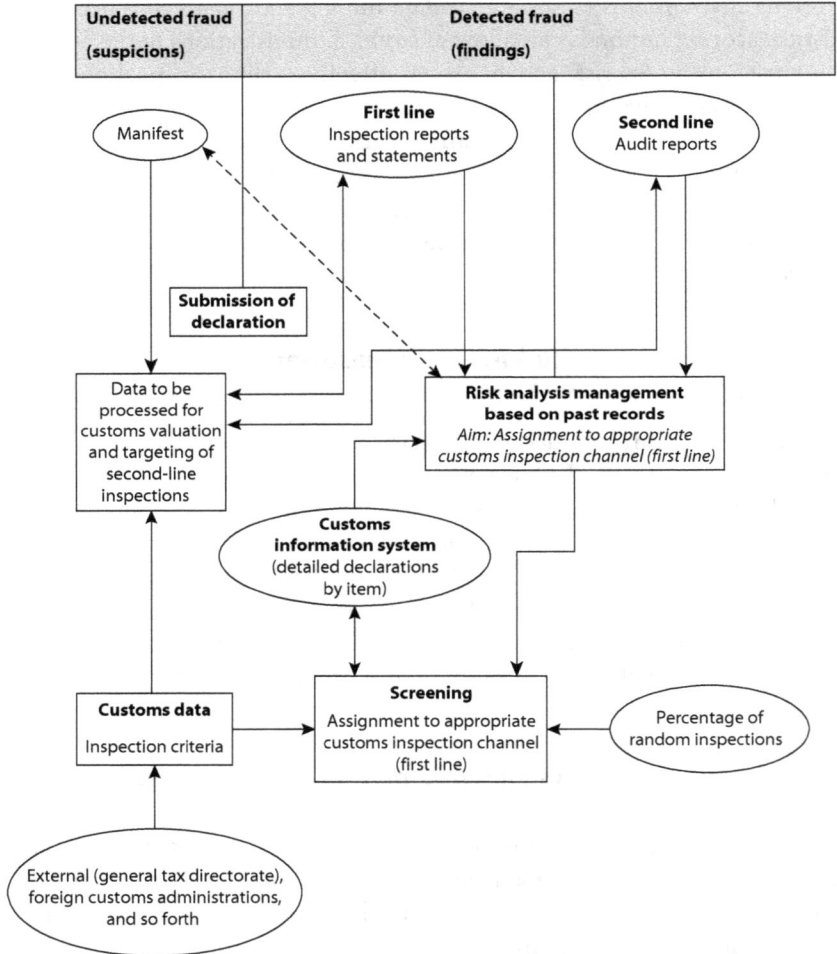

are completed by using available information related to suspected fraud (inspection criteria) and by applying a given percentage of random inspections. The effective operation of the system depends on the quality and use of all of these data. The result leads to the setting up of a data platform that gathers information on detected customs violations and suspected fraud, which are linked item by item to the components of the declarations in question. This platform is at the heart of the overall risk analysis and management system and will facilitate targeting for second-line inspections and assessment of customs violations.

General Architecture of the System: Four Complementary Approaches

The system for targeting declarations for customs inspection should take into account the most important components of a trade transaction: (a) the origin of the goods and the trade channels through which they have passed, (b) the goods that are the object of the trade transaction, and (c) the operators involved in the transaction. The origin and trade channels are important because they may reveal abnormal channels, as determined by knowledge of the most usual and regular trade transactions. The type of goods (which determines tax rates, restrictions, prohibitions, qualitative controls, and special tariff arrangements) and the customs value are two key factors in the presumption of fraud. Finally, the operators involved in the transaction form the remaining component of the system. Although the importer is the main figure involved, there are other operators in the chain (exporter, shipping company, banker, forwarder, and so on).

Using these components, one can design a targeting method by combining four approaches that are based on the statistical analysis of detected cases of fraud and on the incidents of suspected fraud assessed by customs officials, particularly incidents discovered in intelligence-gathering activities. These four approaches are applied iteratively to assign declarations to the appropriate inspection channel.

The first approach involves verifying every new operation that entails an operator, a type of good, or a trade channel for which the customs database supplies no information. These operations should be singled out so that knowledge can be obtained. Crucially, this systematic inspection should prompt the operators to identify themselves correctly, which is essential to customs administration procedures (as well as to tax administration), because postclearance controls should gradually replace import controls at the frontline.

The second approach, which is just as radical as the first, involves systematic inspection of transactions based on factors linked to specific characteristics (for example, transactions of a value greater than x currency units, the fact that the operator has not undergone an inspection in the past x weeks, and so on) and on suspicion of fraud (unconfirmed fraud).

The third approach uses results from an examination of the documents making up the import dossier and the statistical analysis of confirmed cases of fraud to deduce information on the risk of fraud. Each criterion identified (related to trade channels, goods, and operators) is assigned an individual score, which is based on the available statistical data. A representative overall score indicating the fraud risk of the transaction to be inspected is then obtained by combining the individual scores of the various criteria applied.

The fourth approach involves a purely random selection process. It allows customs to limit the number of inspections and is in particular intended to prevent economic operators and unauthorized state officials from modifying their behavior on the basis of statistical information defining the criteria used to detect fraud in the third approach. A significant proportion of the transactions that are singled out for inspection should therefore be selected randomly, especially given that the statistical analysis will initially be based on customs violation data that will be fairly unreliable owing to moral hazard and information asymmetry.

The third approach forms the core of the method because it allows customs to determine the probability of fraud for each transaction on the basis of objective risk criteria identified using statistical inferences. The first step is to determine the fraud criteria through an ex post analysis of confirmed cases of customs violations. The second step is to apply those criteria to each new transaction to determine the probability of fraud (overall score) and, ultimately, the inspection level. Prerequisite to any ex post analysis is the existence of a database of customs violations.

The system's performance depends on the appropriate use of the second and third approaches. The second approach is derived from the analysis of information on fraud that has not yet been confirmed but that has been perceived or suspected by the customs officials in charge of control selectivity. It should allow for coverage of new risks of fraud. The third approach is built on a historical analysis by statisticians of confirmed cases of fraud and an assessment of all known risks over a reference period. Assigning too much importance to the second approach and multiplying the number of criteria that lead to systematic inspection cancels out the benefits derived from carrying out scientific risk analysis.

Statistical Analysis of Confirmed Cases of Fraud

For systems to accurately target the declarations that carry a risk of fraud, data analysis first needs to be carried out. This analysis will involve (a) identifying the characteristics of declarations from the recent past that have involved fraud (a customs violation) and (b) detecting statistical regularities in these incidents of fraudulent behavior (see Laporte 2011). All available information will be used: the content of the certificate of verification produced by the companies in charge of the import verification program, the manifest, the detailed declarations, and the inspection reports (first- and second-line inspections) over the reference period. The statistical regularities identified will be used to outline risk profiles.

Although data are largely qualitative in systems using traditional methods of selectivity, statistical analysis allows the establishment of a quantitative risk scale. For example, to measure the profile of importers, the analyst calculates the frequency of violations for each importer (the ratio of the number of fraudulent declarations by a given importer to the overall number of declarations submitted by that importer over a given period). Importers are then placed on a scale of 0 to 1 (or 0 to 100): 0 for importers that represent no fraud risk, and 1 for importers associated with a high risk of fraud. This type of calculation can be made for all potential risk criteria, including trade channels, operators, and goods, and it can allow the determination of risk profiles for each criterion.

Assignment of a Declaration to a Customs Clearance Channel

The risk profiles obtained are combined to inform decision making with regard to which customs clearance channel a particular declaration should be assigned. The aim is to give each new declaration a score obtained by combining the fraud rates for each of the various criteria. This score should best reflect the risk of fraud, or rather the probability of fraud being committed. Assignment to one of the customs clearance channels is based on this score and on thresholds that were previously determined using statistical analysis.

With the simplest systems, the declaration's score can be obtained by taking a simple or weighted statistical average of the fraud rates (risk profiles) of the various criteria used or simply by taking the highest value from among the criteria (although other combinations can be used). Prior to implementing such a system, the most significant criteria would have been determined in an ad hoc fashion by customs officials responsible for the inspection activities or by statistical trial and error to arrive at the best combinations. The most commonly used criteria are the importer, the shipping agent, the Harmonized System (HS) position, the customs regime, the country of provenance, and the country of origin of the goods. Criteria may also be combined.

More elaborate systems use statistical distribution properties to effectively combine customs data. Econometric models also allow the analyst to identify the risk criteria that best account for an act of fraud and to calculate the probability of fraud for each new declaration. This probability is then the resulting score for the declaration. To perform the calculation, the following equation first needs to be solved using the history of declarations:

$$Pr(Fraud_{ij} = 1) = \alpha + \beta_1 fq_{criterion}1_{ij} + \beta_2 fq_{criterion}2_{ij} + \ldots + \beta_N fq_{criterion}N_{ij} + \varepsilon_{ij},$$

where Pr is the probability; $Fraud_{ij}$ is the binary variable 0/1 for declaration i, product j (1 if fraud and 0 if no fraud); fq_{-ij} is the frequency of fraud for each risk criterion associated with declaration i, product j; ε is the random deviation (that which cannot be explained by the criteria included in the equation); and α and β are the parameters of the equation to be solved.

Experience in West Africa: The Case of Senegal

With the assistance of the International Monetary Fund's West Africa Regional Technical Assistance Center (West AFRITAC), five countries in West Africa are currently developing this type of system: Benin, Burkina Faso, Côte d'Ivoire, Mali, and Senegal. The system has recently been introduced in Benin and Mali and is in a testing phase in Côte d'Ivoire and Senegal. In Burkina Faso, it is just being launched.

Each country has adapted the system to its own context (types of operators, integrated customs clearance systems, involvement of antifraud services, and so on). Thus, Benin was able to develop a statistical scoring system within the ASYCUDA++ (Automated System for Customs Data) computer system, through an econometric analysis of fraud criteria and their various combinations, thanks to technical support funded by external sources.

Mali has circumvented the difficulties associated with a closed computer system (ASYCUDA++) by using statistical risk profiles to assign a risk category (low, medium, or high) to operators, HS positions, and country of origin in its transitional risk analysis and management system. It then combines these risk categories with simple rules to direct declarations to a particular customs clearance channel. For instance, a declaration is assigned to the red channel when two criteria are high risk.

Côte d'Ivoire has developed a transitional system that currently functions in parallel with the SYDAM (Système de Dédouanement Automatisé des Marchandises, or Automated System for Customs Clearance of

Goods) world screening system. When a declaration is assigned the maximum score for the three chosen criteria (importer, HS position, and provenance), it is directed to an inspection channel. The risk analysis is carried out on the basis of the DPI (declaration prior to import)—hence prior to submission of the detailed declaration, which allows inspection services to anticipate the need for inspections.

During the first quarter of 2012, Senegal integrated a two-track system, an automatic risk management system (*Traitement et Analyse de Risque des Marchandeses par Voie Electronique,* or TAMÉ), into Gaindé, its existing system for automatic management of customs information and trade. TAMÉ uses two broad categories of importers: registered and unregistered. Risk analysis for the registered operators is based on the fraud rate for four criteria: importer, country of origin, customs regime, and HS position. Unregistered (occasional) operators are systematically sent for detailed inspection.

Customs Risk Management Previously Applied in Senegal

Customs authorities in Senegal have been applying SIAR (which stands for Système Informatisé d'Analyse de Risque, or Computerized Risk Analysis System), a system developed by the private company Cotecna, to select declarations for inspection. A steering committee for SIAR, comprising representatives from Cotecna and the Senegal customs administration, meets regularly to adapt the system to needs on the ground.

In practice, two risk management systems coexist. The first, SIAR-Senegal, is based on the analysis of data from the import verification program (*programme de vérification des importations,* or PVI) and determines which import shipments should undergo preshipment inspection. The shipments are assigned to one of five inspection channels for destination inspection depending on a certificate of verification. The second risk management system relates to non-PVI imports, which are processed by the Senegal customs administration's Gaindé system, which works on the basis of simple inspection criteria. Thus, 70 percent of imports bypass SIAR-Senegal and are therefore not subjected to the Cotecna risk analysis.

Cotecna SIAR-Senegal. Imports with a free on board (FOB) value of less than CFAF 1 million are excluded from the PVI, which means that importers do not have to submit a DPI. A DPI must be submitted for imports with a cost, insurance, and freight (CIF) value between CFAF 1 million and CFAF 3 million FOB, but they need not undergo preshipment inspection. For DPIs with a value exceeding CFAF 3 million, an inspection is carried out before loading. The certificate of verification is then electronically submitted to the Senegal customs administration using the Gaindé system.

SIAR is organized into two levels: upstream SIAR (*SIAR-amont*) and downstream SIAR (*SIAR-aval*). Upstream SIAR determines the type of intervention undertaken by Cotecna before the goods are loaded. The process, which depends on analysis of the DPI, assigns imports to one of three channels:

- *Blue channel*. Goods are exempted from intervention by Cotecna.
- *Green channel*. A documentary check is required for tariff classification and price analysis.
- *Red channel*. A physical inspection of the goods occurs before loading.

The aim of upstream SIAR is to limit the number of physical preshipment inspections to 10 percent of import transactions. Downstream SIAR determines the type of intervention undertaken by the Senegal customs administration on arrival of goods that have a certificate of verification. It uses five channels:

- *Blue channel*. A release warrant is automatically issued without any inspection, particularly for goods that have undergone a physical preshipment inspection.
- *Green channel*. A documentary check takes place.
- *Yellow channel*. Inspection takes place on the importer's premises.
- *Orange channel*. A documentary check is required, along with inspection by scanning.
- *Red channel*. A physical inspection of goods occurs.

Assignment of the declarations to one of the channels, whether by upstream SIAR or downstream SIAR, is based on a score (econometric model) given to the transaction as well as on the inspection criteria (specific tariff positions, operators, and so on). Cotecna uses its own database, which consists of the results of its own inspections.

How risk is taken into account in Gaindé. For transactions that fall outside the PVI and are therefore not subject to the SIAR risk analysis, the Gaindé system directs the declarations to one of the five inspection channels using only the criteria defined by the SIAR steering committee on the basis of its perception of fraud risk:

- *Blue channel.* This channel is used for changes and goods taken from warehouses.
- *Green channel.* Declarations for perishable products, some suspensive regimes, and importers to whom special arrangements apply use this channel.
- *Yellow channel.* Heavy or dangerous goods as well as personal belongings are tracked through this channel.
- *Orange channel.* Fully loaded containers that fall outside the PVI go through this channel.
- *Red channel.* This channel applies to exemption regimes; products susceptible to fraud; and blacklisted declarants, importers, and countries of origin. It also is used when the value of the goods is higher than a fixed amount as defined by each customs office.

Some general characteristics are common to all the customs offices as well as to local criteria used by individual customs offices, especially for the red channel.

The outcome of all of the controls (SIAR and customs) should, in principle, feed into SIAR to update in real time the risk profiles that form the basis of the statistical scoring. However, this information exchange does not take place, which greatly reduces the effectiveness of this type of system.

Toward a Modern Risk Analysis and Management System Integrated into Gaindé: TAMÉ

Since 2009, the Senegal customs administration has been working to develop its own system of risk analysis and management independent from Cotecna's SIAR and based on its own data.

Prerequisites. The development of a customs risk analysis and management system implies the need for a number of prerequisites, which the Senegal customs administration has gradually put in place. These prerequisites relate to the customs administration's computer system, the institutional framework, and the availability of the data and resources that need to be released. Whereas the customs administrations of other countries use ASYCUDA 2.3 or ++, the Senegal customs administration developed Gaindé, an open system that facilitates in-house development of a risk analysis and management application. The Senegal customs administration's modernization plans identified the risk analysis project as high priority, which led to the creation of a favorable institutional framework—that is, the Analysis and Decision-Making Support

Bureau (Bureau d'Analyse et d'Aide à la Décision, or BAD). The bureau consists of a customs inspector (bureau chief), two statistician-econometricians, and some information technology professionals. A risk management committee was also created, comprising representatives of BAD and the Intelligence and Documentation Bureau (Bureau du Renseignement et de la Documentation). Once constituted, BAD was able to work on compiling a coherent database before conducting the statistical study necessary to develop the system. Finally, the means of execution were put in place for the project both in terms of human resources and financing.

TAMÉ: Initial version. TAMÉ combines the four complementary approaches described previously. Unregistered operators represent about 40 percent of import transactions in Senegal, which led the Senegal customs administration to design a two-track risk analysis and management system whereby importers are divided into two groups, with a different risk management strategy applied to each group (figure 5.2). However, the statistical analysis cannot be applied to unregistered operators because the operator criterion, which plays a major role in determining the overall risk score, does not allow these operators to be distinguished from one another.

The five existing clearance channels are retained in the new system. Version 1.0 of TAMÉ is based on a simple combination of the risk profiles of the four criteria: the importer, the country of provenance, the product (HS code), and the customs regime. Version 2.0 will use econometric analysis to establish which criteria are used and in which combination.

Evaluation of the initial version of TAMÉ: Encouraging first tests. Evaluating the performance of a new risk analysis and management system is difficult because a reference situation to which the targeting outcomes can be compared first needs to be defined. Two reference situations are conceivable: the first would be to compare the targeting outcomes of the new system to those of the existing system, and the second would be to compare the outcomes of the new system to a random selection. However, in either case, it is not easy to carry out the necessary tests because such testing requires that both systems function in parallel, something that is not possible with the integrated customs clearance systems used in most countries. The option that is often chosen is, therefore, the first: comparing the original system with the new system. After all, the aim of the tests is to establish whether,

Figure 5.2   Decision Tree Envisaged by TAMÉ for the Categorization of Declarations

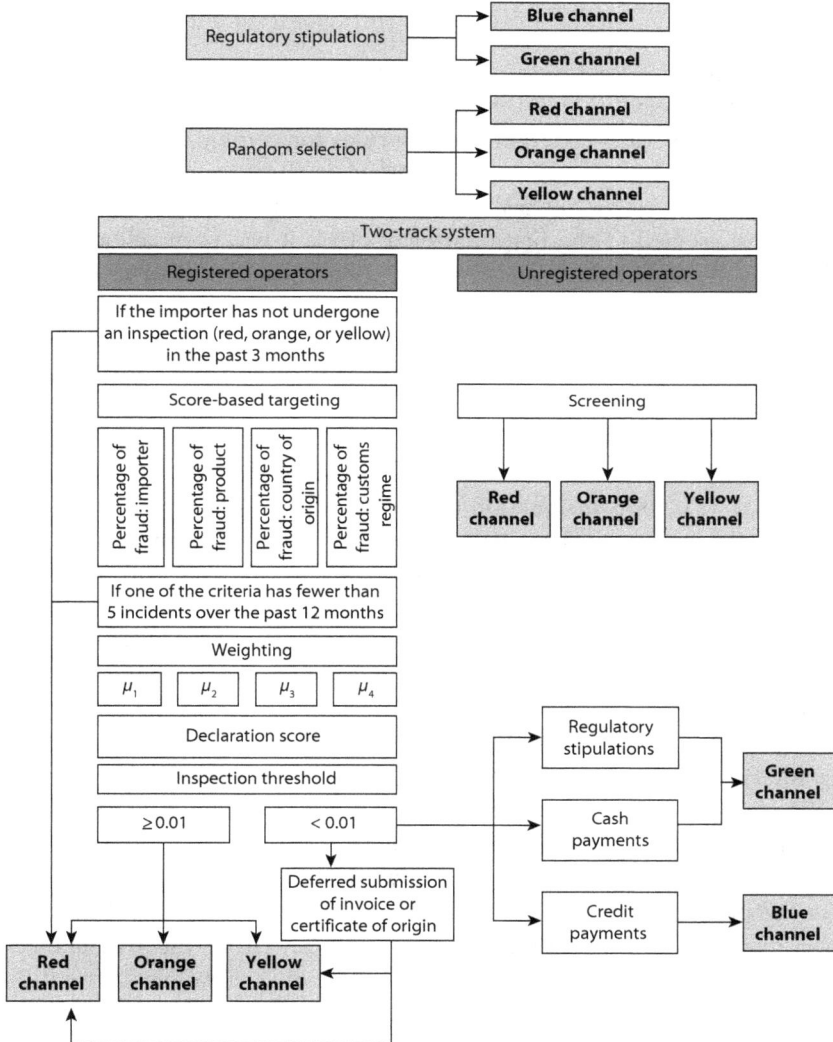

Source: Bureau d'Analyse et d'Aide à la Décision, Senegal Customs Administration.

despite insufficient customs data, the new system is at least as effective at detecting fraud as the old, while inspecting less. What is needed, therefore, is to compare the outcomes of the screening and inspections of the two systems, not in real time but over a given period in the past, with the performance of the new system determined a posteriori. The question that the tests answer is therefore the following: were the violations detected by the old system also detected by the new system but with a lower inspection rate?

The tests carried out for TAMÉ are based on a calibration of the system over four consecutive quarters. That process involved determining the risk profiles for each criterion and the rules for combining them over a given period. The system thus established is then applied to the next quarter. In the case of Senegal, the system was calibrated on the basis of 2010 and applied to the first quarter of 2011; it was then calibrated on the basis of the last three quarters of 2010 and the first quarter of 2011 and applied to the second quarter of 2011. Because the full programming for TAMÉ has not yet been finalized, TAMÉ uses the statistical approach only to determine the risk category of declarations and only for registered operators.

Because the tariff classification is one of the risk assessment criteria, the data are by necessity organized by tariff headings in the database. Hence, if a customs declaration consists of three items, the declaration is divided into three distinct transactions and an overall score is assigned to each of these transactions. The risk classification having been carried out on the basis of the declaration, the classification results are then presented at the declaration level, with the overall risk score assigned to the declaration being equal to the highest score from among distinct transactions.

During the course of the first quarter of 2011, all declarations (7,947 in total) were inspected. They used the red, orange, yellow, and green channels—no declarations were assigned to the blue channel during this period—and were directed to a channel on the basis of either downstream SIAR or Gaindé's criteria. Only 56 of the inspected declarations (or 0.7 percent) were subject to litigation. During the course of the second quarter, 7,633 declarations were inspected (from the red, orange, yellow, and green channels), or 99.8 percent of declarations. A total of 60 declarations (or 0.8 percent) were subject to litigation (see table 5.1). This very low rate of litigation for a high inspection rate is justification enough for developing TAMÉ to improve the effectiveness of risk analysis and management by Senegal customs.

Because the application of TAMÉ in Gaindé has not yet been finalized, only statistical screening has been taken into account in the tests (approach 3 of the system). It distinguishes only two channels: strict inspection channels (red, orange, and yellow) and other channels. The

Table 5.1   Frequency of Detected Fraud among Registered Operators, 2011

	1st quarter		2nd quarter	
Litigation	Number of declarations	Share of declarations (%)	Number of declarations	Share of declarations (%)
No	7,891	99.3	7,573	99.2
Yes	56	0.7	60	0.8
Total	7,947	100.0	7,633	100.0

Source: Bureau d'Analyse et d'Aide à la Décision, Senegal Customs Administration.

Table 5.2   Assignment to Strict Inspection Channels (Red, Orange, and Yellow) and Outcomes of Inspections, 2011

	1st quarter litigation			2nd quarter litigation		
	No	Yes	Share (%)	No	Yes	Share (%)
SIAR and Gaindé	5,192	34	0.65	4,812	45	0.93
SAGAR	2,004	28	1.38	1,368	24	1.72

Source: Bureau d'Analyse et d'Aide à la Décision, Senegal Customs Administration.

results outlined in table 5.2, therefore, reflect only the channels common to both systems—that is, the detailed inspection channels for which the outcomes are known.

In the first quarter of 2011, downstream SIAR and Gaindé assigned 5,192 declarations to the red, orange, and yellow channels. Among them, only 34 were subject to litigation, a litigation rate of 0.65 percent. TAMÉ would have assigned only 2,004 declarations to the same channels—that is, a 60 percent reduction in inspections. Among those assigned to the red, orange, and yellow channels, 28 of the 34 declarations that were subject to litigation were targeted, which would have produced a litigation rate of 1.38 percent. In the second quarter, SIAR and Gaindé assigned 4,812 declarations to the red, orange, and yellow channels, of which 45 were subject to litigation, or a litigation rate of 0.93 percent. TAMÉ would have assigned only 1,368 declarations to the same channels—that is, a reduction in inspections of more than 70 percent. Among those assigned, 24 of the 45 declarations that were subject to litigation were targeted, producing a litigation rate of 1.72 percent—only a slightly worse result than that in the first quarter.

These results are particularly interesting. In the first quarter, TAMÉ detected more than 80 percent of the declarations that were subject to litigation while reducing the number of inspections by a factor of more than 2.6. Moreover, this result was achieved with TAMÉ's targeting mechanism, which uses only one of the four approaches making up the risk analysis and management system. Taking into account the other three should therefore allow TAMÉ to identify virtually all the cases of fraud revealed by SIAR and Gaindé but with a significantly reduced number of inspections. Moreover, reducing the number of inspections should improve the quality of the inspections carried out and, hence, the detection of additional cases of fraud.

Data Mining: An Accelerator for Customs Modernization

The experiments carried out in West Africa have helped to address some doubts with regard to the usefulness of this type of technique in administrations that have limited resources but are already undertaking far-reaching reforms. The results of this study raise two questions. First, can this type of sophisticated system be developed in these administrations? Second, is it appropriate to dedicate time and resources to the development of data-mining and scoring techniques far removed from the purely customs-related concerns of the numerous activities already undertaken (combating fraud, assessing value, and so forth)?

First of all, the weakness of customs administrations does not represent an obstacle to the development of this type of system. On the contrary, some aspects of the dysfunctionality within these administrations, including the lack of ethics, are directly addressed by the use of scientific risk analysis techniques that remove the need to rely on decision making based on human judgment. In addition, most customs administrations already have the skills necessary to apply these techniques, although capacities related to data mining and statistical inference may need to be strengthened.

Investing in the development of these techniques contributes significantly, either directly or indirectly, to the modernization process in the customs administrations that choose to adopt them.

Direct Effects on the Reform Process

In itself, risk analysis provides powerful leverage for the general reform of customs administrations, particularly because it requires closer cooperation between the various services in charge of inspections and intelligence. Limiting the number of first-line inspections also frees up inspectors, who can be redeployed to carry out postclearance audits. The development of this type of inspection, which has been virtually nonexistent until now, represents an important component of any reform program.

The prerequisite for using data mining to assess the risk of fraud is the compilation of a reliable database of customs violations. Because it is essential to ensure the traceability of instances of detected fraud at every level (both first and second line), this effort implies computerizing customs litigation—that is, making it possible for records to be created online and fines to be issued electronically. Customs administrations that have adopted this approach have been led to completely review all their litigation procedures before computerizing them, which allowed the procedures to be simplified. This process drew attention to a number of profound dysfunctions. It also represented an opportunity to bring together information technology specialists, statisticians, and customs inspectors and to have them work together through a rigorous approach conducive to the adoption of new technologies.

Structural Change in the Culture of Customs Administrations
The use of data mining brings about a significant change in attitudes and behavior. One of the foundations of a modern customs administration is information. If customs administrations gather or have access to a large amount of data, these data are often scattered, compartmentalized, incomplete, and as a result, difficult to mine. Moreover, when data exist, they are generally poorly used or not used at all. The approach taken by the customs authorities that took part in these experiments created an awareness of the importance of using data over and above the specific aim of developing a risk analysis and management system. It allowed these administrations to realize the value of specific tasks, including the production of monitoring indicators. This change in culture can facilitate the achievement of the modernization program's objectives, particularly with regard to management of human resources and management of the system overall.

A Doorway to Other Projects
The development of risk analysis and management systems using data mining should open up new possibilities for other innovative modernization projects, including, for example, the categorization of operators and the introduction of performance contracts.

Defining the main categories of the customs administration's clients is essential to adapting procedures and controls, especially when the aim is to make these elements more efficient. The analytical results obtained with regard to importer risk make up a natural part of the criteria that need to be met for these importers to be granted the status of "authorized economic operator," as advocated by the World Customs Organization and World Trade Organization. The results are also useful in establishing lists of high-risk operators when combined with other criteria.[2] The categorization of operators then allows for the adaptation of screening procedures according to risk. In theory, authorized economic operators are never directed to the red channel except in the rare cases when they are randomly selected, in which case they are obliged to submit their goods to inspection. Operators considered very high risk are almost always directed to the red channel because being classified as high risk represents an inspection criterion. It is for the other operators that risk analysis and management system plays the most significant role, when it determines whether to direct those operators to the red channel (about 20 percent of them are so directed).

Documentary checks are traditionally carried out for products that are not assigned to the red channel and for which regulations require that specific documents be produced.

Recently, the customs administration in Cameroon launched a pilot program for performance contracts that had very positive outcomes with regard to reducing customs clearance delays, mobilizing revenue, and improving officials' behavior (Cantens and others 2011). These performance contracts aim to promote a results-based culture in the administration by outlining objectives that reflect the expected results. This new approach depends on the quantification and evaluation of indicators and thus requires access to the necessary data. The development of risk analysis systems based on data mining, which implies the availability of a set of data on fraud, is based on the same philosophy and should open the way to this type of experiment in the customs administrations of other African countries.

Conclusion

Risk analysis is indispensable for customs administrations in developing countries whose goal is to carry out fewer, more effective inspections. These administrations have recently come to realize the possibilities offered by data mining, thanks to initiatives by the inspection companies that proposed using the results of tools they developed for their own screening procedures. However, customs administrations have not been able to appropriate these tools, and they now feel the need to develop this type of system in-house. Over the past five years, five countries in West Africa have launched projects in this regard with the support of West AFRITAC and the International Monetary Fund. Each administration has adopted an approach that was tailored to its context and its needs, and significant progress has been achieved. In the case of Senegal, a comparison between the results of the targeted system that uses data mining to assess risk and the results of the traditional screening system demonstrate the progress made with regard to trade facilitation. In addition, these experiments show the positive effects of these projects on the reform process through their direct effect on work procedures and methods, the development of an information culture, and the opening of a way toward other innovative projects.

Notes

1. See article VIII of the General Agreement on Tariffs and Trade, which aims to limit the number of procedures required for import and export operations.
2. In addition to occasional operators, high-risk operators can be identified by analyzing the file of taxpayers to identify suspicious operators (for instance, operators that match several names or from whom tax has not been collected on any activity for the past fiscal year).

References

Cantens, Thomas, Gaël Raballand, Nicholas Strychacz, and Tchapa Tchouawou. 2011. "Réforme des douanes africaines: Les résultats des contrats de performance au Cameroun." Africa—Trade Policy Note 13, World Bank, Washington, DC.

Dequiedt, Vianney, Anne-Marie Geourjon, and Grégoire Rota Graziosi. 2009. "Les programmes de vérification des importations (PVI) à la lumière de la théorie de l'agence." Afrique Contemporaine 230 (2): 151–66.

———. 2012. "Mutual Supervision in Preshipment Inspection Programs." Journal of Development Economics 99 (2): 282–91.

Gates, Stephen. 2006. "Incorporating Strategic Risk into Enterprise Risk Management: A Survey of Current Corporate Practices." Journal of Applied Corporate Finance 18 (4): 81–90.

Geourjon, Anne-Marie, Grégoire Rota Graziosi, and Bertrand Laporte. 2010. "Comment moderniser l'analyse du risque et la sélectivité des contrôles douaniers dans les pays en développement?" OMD Actualités 62: 29–31.

Geourjon, Anne-Marie, and Bertrand Laporte. 2005. "Risk Management for Targeting Customs Controls in Developing Countries: A Risky Venture for Revenue Performance?" *Public Administration and Development* 25 (2): 105–13.

Grigoriou, Christopher. 2012. "How Can Risk Management Help Enforce Technical Measures?" In *Non-tariff Measures: A Fresh Look at Trade Policy's New Frontier*, ed. Olivier Cadot and Mariem Malouche, 283–96. Washington, DC: World Bank.

Harrison, Mark, and Steve Holloway. 2007. "Customs and Supply Chain Security: 'The Demise of Risk Management?'" Paper presented at the Asia-Pacific Economic Cooperation's Annual Conference of APEC Centers, Melbourne, Australia, April 18–20.

Hintsa, Juha, Toni Männistö, Ari-Pekka Hameri, Christopher Thibedeau, Jukka Sahlstedt, Vladlen Tsikolenko, Matthias Finger, and Mikael Granqvist. 2011. "Customs Risk Management (CRiM): A Survey of 24 WCO Member Administrations." Cross-Border Research Association; École Polytechnique Fédérale de Lausanne; and Hautes Études Commerciales, Université de Lausanne, Lausanne, Switzerland.

Laporte, Bertrand. 2011. "Risk Management Systems: Using Data Mining in Developing Countries' Customs Administrations." *World Customs Journal* 5 (1): 17–27.

Walsh, James T. 2003. "Post-release Verification and Audit." In *Changing Customs: Challenges and Strategies for the Reform of Customs Administration*, ed. Michael Keen, 74–82. Washington, DC: International Monetary Fund.

WCO (World Customs Organization). 2003. "Guide sur la gestion des risques." Brussels.

Widdowson, David. 2005. "Managing Risk in the Customs Context." In *Customs Modernization Handbook*, ed. Luc De Wulf and José B. Sokol, 91–99. Washington, DC: World Bank.

CHAPTER 6

Mirror Trade Statistics: A Tool to Help Identify Customs Fraud

A Cameroon Case Study

Gaël Raballand, Thomas Cantens, and Guillermo Arenas

This chapter analyzes detailed data and information on Cameroon's imports to identify sectors where the likelihood of customs undervaluation (or overvaluation) is the highest, hence offering an additional tool for customs officers to better develop their risk management policy and implement cargo selectivity. *Mirror statistics* is the use of partner trade statistics to assess trade patterns of country X. Used extensively in international economics for several decades, this method has regularly demonstrated that high taxes act as an incentive to increase tariff evasion and misclassification.[1]

A seminal article by Bhagwati (1964) explained that, in the case of Turkey, the categories of goods that showed the most important "perverse discrepancies" had tariff rates ranging up to 30 percent and rarely below 10 percent. Bhagwati (1967) also used mirror statistics to demonstrate the effect of undervaluation and overvaluation of trade statistics on balance-of-payments data.

Pritchett and Sethi (1994) used data on items in the tariff code from three developing countries—Jamaica, Kenya, and Pakistan—to examine the relationship between tariff revenues and tariff rates. They demonstrated that collected revenues and official tariff rates are only weakly related and, even more interesting, that the variance of collected rates increases strongly with the level of the official rate. Finally, they found weak evidence showing that beyond a certain limit, further increases in the official tariff rate produce no increase (and perhaps a decrease) in the collected rate.

Using mirror statistics, Fisman and Wei (2004) quantified the effects of tax rates on tax evasion in China by examining the relationship between the tariff schedule and the evasion gap, which they defined as the difference between reported exports of Hong Kong SAR, China, to the rest of China at the product level and China's reported imports from Hong Kong SAR, China. They found that a 1 percentage point increase in the tax rate is associated with a 3 percent increase in evasion and that evasion takes place partly through misclassification of imports from higher-taxed categories to lower-taxed ones, in addition to underreporting the value of imports.

Focusing more on Central and Eastern European countries, Javorcik and Narciso (2007) found that differentiated products may be subject to greater tariff evasion because of the difficulties associated with assessing their quality and price. Moreover, greater tariff evasion observed for differentiated products tends to take place through misrepresentation of the import prices (and not through quantity or undervaluation).

Trade economists have used mirror statistics to demonstrate trade data reliability problems. In this regard, Yeats (1978) pointed out problems with trade statistics, especially at the disaggregated level. He explained that discrepancies in lower-level trade statistics are often considerable and suggested the desirability of more fully assessing the trade-off between level of disaggregation and reliability of the underlying data.

More recently, mirror statistics are increasingly used at a detailed level for customs analysis. Taking the example of the Kyrgyz Republic and using information on the ground about bazaar development, Kaminski and Raballand (2009) used mirror statistics to demonstrate how the Kyrgyz Republic had become a reexport platform for Chinese consumer goods going to Central Asia. In the same vein, Raballand and Mjekiqi (2010) used mirror statistics (and port traffic data) to evaluate the extent of smuggling to Nigeria (through Benin) attributable to import prohibitions.

Despite their interest, most of these papers have not been used primarily to help customs officers reduce fraud. That is where this chapter is different, because it was designed to be used for customs and is a tool to help Cameroon Customs better monitor fraud practices. Proof of tariff evasion is difficult to find, but mirror statistics appear to help in the following ways:

- To understand a fraud mechanism
- To evaluate the effect of customs controls and management when new measures are undertaken to fight fraud (in one case, the gap strongly decreased when a new head of a customs bureau was appointed)
- To unveil the bargaining process used by some customs officers with traders and importers
- To evaluate revenue losses
- To generate political will from customs management

This experiment is ongoing in Cameroon, but preliminary results and lessons can be shared at this stage. The tool was designed in two steps: analysis using mirror statistics and then consultations with customs officials in charge of risk analysis and operational offices to improve revenue collection and decrease fraud. This chapter demonstrates how useful mirror statistics can be for customs field officers.

First, this chapter compares, in value and weight, (a) exports to Cameroon reported in the United Nations Commodity Trade Statistics Database (UN Comtrade) and (b) imports reported in the Cameroon Customs database from 2007 to 2010. This first step made systematic comparisons and identified the largest discrepancies with the highest potential for fraud and revenue effects. Some of the discrepancies were ignored by customs officers; others were known, but the extent of fraud was not known. The second step investigated some specific flows of goods to unveil how fraud is organized and to provide information that would improve controls on the ground.

In the chapter's second section, database characteristics are discussed together with the limitations on this type of exercise. Then some product examples in the case of Cameroon are presented. Lessons to take into account for low-governance countries are described, and a final section presents areas for further research.

Data Accuracy and Methodological Issues

Limits to the accuracy of mirror statistics have been well known for several decades.

Data Accuracy Issues

In this regard, Bhagwati (1964) points out the three main explanations of discrepancies in trade statistics, but also demonstrates that when discrepancies are above 20 to 30 percent, which is the case for Cameroon, fraud or evasion can be presumed.

The first plausible explanation of the discrepancy is just an error of commodity classification. This case is considered marginal.

The second explanation is a time lag between exports and import declarations. This difference may be an issue, but it should even out over time (if there is no underinvoicing or overinvoicing). From China, travel time for goods to Douala, Cameroon, is 45 days; from the European Union (EU), the time is two weeks, and the lag is therefore rather limited and cannot explain important differences. Moreover, any gaps detected for 2010 were computed on the former years as well to limit the potential gap due to the time lag between exports and import declarations.

The third explanation is obviously transport costs, but differences for some commodities are so large that they cannot explain mirror statistics discrepancies.[2] For this reason, we have computed differences in weights over several years to have a second factor that may or may not be able to explain mirror statistics discrepancies.

The fourth explanation is what Bhagwati (1964) called "misallocation" of imports: imports can be wrongly attributed to Belgium, for example, when they were manufactured in France and only traded through a Belgian port. To limit this problem, EU countries were aggregated, and the same was done for China and Hong Kong SAR, China. Moreover, we aggregate transit and import declarations because one exporter can declare that the destination country is Cameroon when the real one is Chad. Nevertheless, ASYCUDA (Automated System for Customs Data) makes a distinction between origin and provenance, and we combined both to avoid this problem.

The fifth explanation would be exchange rate volatility, because data are converted on a yearly average. Therefore, substantial exchange rate appreciation or depreciation could possibly bias some trade data.

The final issue would be undervaluation from the exporting country and a simultaneous undervaluation of imports by the importing country. In such a case, nothing would be detected, but this study identified several major discrepancies. One just needs to keep in mind that (a) for operational purposes, the existence of discrepancies is more important than the accuracy of the discrepancies themselves when they are large, and (b) the measured gaps are minimal and are probably greater than what was identified.

UN Comtrade

Mirror analysis compares export data extracted from UN Comtrade and import data extracted from ASYCUDA Cameroon. Using UN Comtrade allows several kinds of comparisons at different levels of aggregation: six-, four-, and two-digit levels of the Harmonized System (HS). Concerning Cameroon and its major import flows, most UN Comtrade data used are provided by China, the EU, and the United States. Mirror data were compiled from the UN Comtrade database using WITS (World Integrated Trade Solution) software. Each product is defined at the HS six-digit level using the HS 2007 nomenclature. Values are recorded in millions of U.S. dollars, and quantities are presented in several units, depending on the reporting country (kilograms, number of items, square meters, and liters, among others). Unlike the Cameroon Customs database, the mirror database does not provide information on quantities for a relatively large share of imports.[3] The mirror database contains 56,469 entries that represent imports by Cameroon of 4,042 products from 109 countries for the 2007–10 period.

All import flows in the customs database cannot be matched because some of Cameroon's partners do not report to UN Comtrade.[4] The total import values in both databases differ significantly and do not follow the same trends. In this case, differences had more to do with how many countries were reporting for a particular year than other factors. Particularly, the smaller difference observed after 2009 is in part because Nigeria reported data to UN Comtrade in 2009 and 2010 but not in 2007 and 2008.

Comparison of imports at the country level seems more promising, but some discrepancies remain. In some countries, namely the 27 EU member states (EU-27)[5] and China, customs and mirror databases follow each other, and differences are relatively small. In other countries, some important differences remain and trends are not similar (for example, Japan, Thailand, and the United States). Imports from Japan and Thailand show the highest differences in relative terms. The fact that the global gap between one trade partner and Cameroon is small does not necessarily give any information on the fiscal dimension, because gaps in an HS chapter may partly compensate.

Cameroon Customs Database

The Cameroon Customs database has information on import values and quantities by product and country of origin from 2007 to 2010.[6] Each product is defined at the HS 11-digit level using the HS 2007 nomenclature. Values are recorded in millions of CFAF (Communauté Financière

Africaine, or African Financial Community francs), which is the currency of Cameroon, and quantities are presented in both kilograms and number of items for each product. Each of the 147,728 entries in the customs database represents an imported product from a country in a particular year. The entries in the customs database represent imports of 4,988 products from 203 countries for the 2007–10 period.

The most detailed level at which international comparisons of trade flows can be conducted is the HS six-digit level. More detailed disaggregation (for example, the HS 11-digit level) is based on country-specific HS lines and may not be comparable between countries. Thus, the original customs data were recoded at the HS six-digit level. After collapsing values and quantities at the HS six-digit level, the customs database has 116,610 entries, representing imports of 4,600 products and 176 countries for the 2007–10 period.[7]

Comparison of Reported Quantities in the Customs and Mirror Databases

Comparing imported quantities between the customs and mirror databases is more troublesome. Although the customs database provides quantity data in kilograms for all products, the mirror database does not. Reporting of quantity units to the UN Comtrade database is not homogeneous, and the reporting units depend on the country—and can vary from year to year for the same country. Some countries report quantities in units other than kilograms (such as number of items, square meters, and liters) or simply do not report quantity units for some items.

Thus, only products for which a particular country reported quantities in kilograms to UN Comtrade could be matched with customs quantities. Matching other products would require transformation ratios from other measures to kilograms. Table 6.1 shows the percentage of import values that are reported in kilograms for the top 10 countries in the mirror database.

Quantity reporting in kilograms may be complemented by "supplementary units" reporting, which are units of products, such as the number of vehicles. This type of reporting is especially important for motorcycles and spare parts.

The customs and mirror databases were merged after cleaning the data following the steps previously described. Import values are originally recorded in U.S. dollars in the mirror database and were converted to CFA francs using the exchange rate from the World Bank's World Development Indicators database.

Table 6.1   Percentage of Import Value Reported in Kilograms in the Mirror Database

Top 10 countries	2007	2008	2009	2010
France	70	72	69	71
China	44	50	56	55
United States	21	32	74	69
Germany	50	54	55	44
Belgium	67	62	61	65
Japan	24	25	32	34
Thailand	91	90	94	96
Italy	60	62	63	64
Brazil	—	98	92	94
Netherlands	77	76	65	—

Source: UN Comtrade and Cameroon Customs database.
Note: — = no mirror data available.

The Main Findings of the Cameroon Case Study

The differences are calculated as customs values minus mirror values. Several examples are presented, illustrating various probable fraud mechanisms. More cases were detected, but for some of them, suspicions were not necessarily confirmed through discussions with operational customs officers.

For confidentiality reasons, the HS headings and subheadings of the commodities are kept anonymous.

Case 1: Attractive Subheadings in a Chapter: Subheadings That Are More Taxed and That Have a Threshold Value

The first example is the subheading X1 (manufactured goods), which is heavily taxed (at 30 percent, the highest tariff rate), with a minimum value imposed by the administration. These goods are imported mostly from one country.

In UN Comtrade, China's export flows are prevalent: Chinese exports represent 89 percent of total exports (table 6.2).

The threshold value (set by Cameroon Customs) is higher than the declared value for exports (134 percent of exports value, which could be explained by transportation costs). The main issue concerns large differences in quantities and values. Moreover, this trend has increased every year since 2007: between 1,000 and 2,000 metric tons "disappear" between declared exports from China and declared imports in Cameroon. By applying the Chinese declared quantity and the threshold value, one would

Table 6.2   Quantity, Value, and Value Density for Products from China

Data source	Quantity (metric tons)	Value (CFAF millions)	Value density (CFAF/kilogram)
UN Comtrade data	2,360	7,253	3,072
Cameroonian import data (origin or China provenance)	90	380	4,217 (equal to the minimum value)

Source: World Bank.

expect the imported values in 2010 to have been CFAF 9,952 million, which represents potential additional duties and taxes of CFAF 5,473 billion (or over 50 percent of total declared values).

This analysis has been conducted on the subheading HS6 and can be extended to the whole HS chapter (HS2). Two subheadings within the chapter, Y1 and Z1, are taxed at 20 percent (instead of 30 percent) and have large import volumes, which may raise questions because they are subject to large exemptions and are taxed at a lower rate.

According to Cameroon Customs data in 2010, 30 percent of Cameroon's imports of goods for the chapter came from Y1, imported from Benin, but these goods were not manufactured in Benin. This category is taxed at 20 percent, it has no threshold, and the average value of imports is CFAF 672 per kilogram (compared with more than CFAF 3,000 per kilogram for category X1). Benin export data for 2009 and 2010 do not appear in UN Comtrade. Moreover, virtually no country in the world seems to have exported this product to Benin, Cameroon, and Nigeria in 2009 and 2010. In addition, four import operations for this tariff position were subject to exemptions.

Moreover, according to Cameroonian data in 2010, 34 percent of Cameroon's imported goods in the chapter came from China in the tariff line Z1. This position is taxed at 20 percent, it has no threshold, and the average value of imports is CFAF 281 per kilogram. China's declared exports weighed 254 metric tons in 2010, but according to Cameroon Customs data, 999 metric tons were imported. In addition, six import transactions of this subheading have given rise to exemptions.

In conclusion, two assumptions are likely, and they are not mutually exclusive:

- X1 is smuggled, undeclared, which causes a potential loss of revenues of CFAF 5.5 billion (or approximately CFAF 11 million of CFAF 14 million declared for exports).

- X1 is imported under false declarations under the subheadings with lower tariff rates (Y1 and Z1) and is subject to exemptions from duties and taxes except for the quantities that remain lower than the observed deviation of subheading X1.

The second example is food products (O1–O18) that have a similar appearance, the same packaging, and sometimes the same use and that are classified within the same chapter, including subheadings taxed from 10 percent to 30 percent, with some minimum values set by the administration (see annex 6A for details). Using data extracted from annex 6A, we can conclude the following:

- Minimal threshold values are all much higher than declared export prices.
- All low-taxed goods record a positive gap, which means they are probably misclassifications.
- A loss is recorded for two positions subject to minimal prices (O8 and O16), with a gap of 8,000 metric tons. The 8,000 metric tons are likely declared under the subheading O7, which is taxed at 30 percent but with a density value of CFAF 480 per kilogram (instead of CFAF 1,500 per kilogram). The shortfall is therefore approximately CFAF 6,684 billion for 2010, from which we need to subtract CFAF 2,143 billion for duties and taxes paid under the position O7. The real loss would then be approximately US$4.5 billion (or almost US$10 million if the misclassification were complete between O8 and O16 to O7).

The third example is a raw commodity, M1–M3. One can review the position of goods taxed differently with no minimum value set out in the subtariff. The subheadings of M1 are taxed differently and record significant differences in export quantity from some countries (table 6.3).

For M3, a specific analysis was conducted for each export country. This analysis shows that a significant fraud may have spread from the United States, because the United States reported CFAF 1,017 million for exports to Cameroon for M3, whereas Cameroon declared CFAF 1 million to CFAF 2 million of M3 from the United States.

Case 2: Misclassification with Low-Taxed Subpositions (Spare Parts) of Another Subposition Taxed at a Higher Rate

The fourth example, X2, is a manufactured good, heavily taxed and imported mostly from one country. According to UN Comtrade, China

Table 6.3   Quantity, Value, and Value Density for M1–M3

HS6	Duty (%)	UN Comtrade	Cameroon Customs data	Loss
M1	5	CFAF 7,746 million	CFAF 7,985 million	
		2,491 metric tons	2,700 metric tons	
		CFAF 3,109/kilogram	CFAF 2,944/kilogram	
M2	30	CFAF 166 million	CFAF 17 million	CFAF 80 million
		123 metric tons	13 metric tons	
		CFAF 1,351/kilogram	CFAF 1,355/kilogram	
M3	10 or 30	CFAF 4,705 million	CFAF 3,290 million	CFAF 775 million
		11,713 metric tons	8,256 metric tons	
		CFAF 402/kilogram	CFAF 398/kilogram	

Source: UN Comtrade and Cameroon Customs database.

Table 6.4   Quantity, Value, and Value Density for X2 from China

Database		Quantity (metric tons)	Value (CFAF millions)	Value density (CFAF/unit)
Chinese data (UN Comtrade)		1,658 (80,144 units)	14,460	180,436
Cameroon data	For home consumption and international transit[a]	5,885 (70,287 units)	9,143	130,081
	For home consumption only	5,417 (60,250 units)	8,078	134,091

Source: UN Comtrade and Cameroon Customs database.
a. Transit for home consumption and international transit have been merged to ensure that the discrepancy is not due to mistakes in the declaration of destination in the export country. In this case, even when merged, the import flows are undervalued.

exports about US$30 million per year of X2 to Cameroon, representing 94 percent of total X2 exports to Cameroon. The second-largest exporter is India with US$0.9 million in X2 exports. Chinese data on quantities are expressed in weight estimates from standard values (table 6.4).

This subheading has two main problems. The first is the unit value imported, which is about 30 percent lower than the value declared for export. By applying a threshold value of CFAF 185,000 per unit and keeping the number of units declared for import in Cameroon similar, one would expect the value to be CFAF 11.1 billion, an increase of CFAF 3 billion over what is declared. This value would lead to additional duties and taxes of CFAF 1.671 billion (over US$3 million).

The quantity reported shows the same problem. In terms of units, the declared gap is 30 percent, which represents a potential loss of

Table 6.5   Value and Total Duties and Taxes for Spare Parts Y2 from China

Data source	Value (CFAF millions)	Duties and taxes (CFAF millions)
Cameroon data		
With partial exemption	2,900	788
Without exemption	674	289
Chinese data for exports	610	262
Duties and taxes subject to misclassification		= 788 + 289 − 262 = 815

Source: World Bank.

CFAF 1.3 billion of taxes and duties (over US$2.5 million). If these computations are combined, the declared value should be around CFAF 14 billion instead of CFAF 8 billion, and the additional duties and taxes should be CFAF 3.3 billion in 2010.

The analysis can be refined by taking into account Y2, spare parts of X2 (table 6.5). Most likely X2 has been misclassified as Y2, the latter of which is taxed at 20 percent instead of 30 percent.

According to information from the field, some X2 units are likely imported disassembled. Indeed, exported values to Cameroon for Y2 parts are CFAF 610 million. In contrast, imported values declared in Cameroon are CFAF 4.195 million. If some imports are misclassified, the overall tax loss is the shortfall on X2 less duties and taxes paid for Y2. The tax loss would be equal to CFAF 2,485 million in 2010 (almost US$5 million).

Case 3: Overvaluation

This fifth example is raw material used for the food industry. The analysis has been conducted at HS4 level because subheadings for goods are taxed identically and there is no minimum value. The analysis found a positive gap.

The subheadings are all taxed at 10 percent. Imports mostly involve a few economic operators who are important contributors to customs revenues. Interestingly, mirror statistics reveal an overvaluation with a positive gap in favor of Cameroon (see table 6.6).

Moving to the whole chapter, we identify a gap equal to CFAF 16 billion (over US$30 million). This gap is the same as the one formerly detected for the heading HS4. In such a case, examining each importer's imports is worthwhile to detect whether overvaluation is systemic. About 200 import operations took place in 2010, which were undertaken by a few importers.

Table 6.6   Quantity, Value, and Value Density for a Raw Material

Exporter	UN Comtrade	Cameroon Customs
Total	CFAF 13,572 million	CFAF 28,226 million
	71,685 metric tons	77,063 metric tons
	CFAF 189/kilogram	CFAF 366/kilogram
Belgium	CFAF 5,812 million	Close to CFAF 300/kilogram
	31,110 metric tons	
	CFAF 187/kilogram	
France	CFAF 4,881 million	
	26,502 metric tons	
	CFAF 184/kilogram	

Source: World Bank.
Note: Data for Cameroon ara computed globally for the EU.

Imports of the first importer represented 81 percent of total import volumes (for a density value of around CFAF 400 per kilogram). Therefore, transfer pricing to evade taxes on profits in Cameroon seems possible, because the quantity seems to be rather similar.

The Main Lessons of the Cameroon Case Study

This chapter presents the first step of an experiment in risk analysis design. Most of these cases are connected to a specific control, either ex-post or on the ground. On the basis of this case study, the following lessons can be applied to future studies in this area for developing countries:

- *Ensure that the tariff complies with the valid HS version.* This task is not easy. Rozanski and Yeats (1994) explained that although the shift toward the Harmonized System was intended to impart a greater degree of data precision, two difficulties may have produced an opposite effect. First, some developing countries were not adequately prepared for the new compilation procedures, and their national statistics could not be matched satisfactorily with the new Standard International Trade Classification when the transition began. Second, some governments were not fully aware of disclosure problems associated with the shift to the HS. Once these problems surfaced, some transactions were intentionally not reported to preserve confidentiality. Use of the HS coding system is therefore problematic in some countries.

- *Aggregate export data for all countries exporting to the destination country for any product where a gap seems important.* Given a lack of supplier diversification, capturing aggregated gaps is important because imports may be misallocated from one country to another. Import declarations can sometimes confuse countries of origin and provenance. The consequence is that, for the same product, a positive gap can be identified with one EU country and a negative gap with another. This problem often occurs in the case of goods that originate in the EU and are exported through Belgium. It is simple to avoid, however, because the UN Comtrade database has an aggregated category for EU countries. The same problem might arise for supply chains that are linked to Middle East countries, especially the United Arab Emirates. Evidence exists that some Cameroonian traders buy goods from East Asia through Dubai suppliers.

• *Compute gaps in goods' density value (value/weight or more units) in addition to differences in absolute weight and quantity.* This exercise is particularly useful for tariff headings for which customs sets minimal values, because the minimal value may be respected but not the weight.

• *Compute separately the largest positive and negative gaps.* In the case of misclassified goods, a commodity is fraudulently declared on several subheadings, which leads to positive and negative gaps for the same product.

• *Be flexible in the analysis.* Fraud mechanisms vary from one product to another; therefore no clear-cut methodology applies. (Fraud can take place within a same HS chapter or between chapters.)

This analysis guides priorities for operational controls by classifying the importance of revenue losses, which is impossible with nonquantified methodologies. Interviewed officers tend to focus on fraud cases for which a single case was important rather than on rampant fraud applied to many imports; however, in most cases, rampant fraud involves larger amounts than nonrampant fraud.

Conclusion and Areas for Further Research

This chapter demonstrates that by identifying about 10 targeted products, fraud can be estimated to the magnitude of 10 to 20 percent of current collected revenues in Cameroon (equivalent to more than US$50 million).

As mentioned previously, because of statistical issues, the amount should not be taken at face value, and a second, more operational, step should be undertaken to further investigate and control. From our point of view, the existence of a gap is more important than its accuracy.

A preliminary stage of systematic comparison is essential to identify patterns of fraud not based solely on empirical knowledge. The second stage is to investigate specific cases to explain the discrepancies by unveiling precise fraud processes or to uncover potential import flows that may hide fraud. Operational units seem to find this type of analysis extremely useful, especially in the case of minimal threshold values, because they may have been fooled by importers who declare a higher value per kilogram but "forget" to declare the metric tons involved, thus making customs face huge revenue losses.

In conclusion, this tool, even though it should be taken with caution, seems to have a bright future when used with operational customs units to better quantify and identify systematic customs fraud.

Annex 6A: Statistical Data for the Food Products Example

Table 6A.1 shows the statistical data underlying the food products (O1–O18) example.

Table 6A.1 Quantity, Value, Value Density, Tariff Duties Percentage, and Existence of a Threshold for O1–O18

Subheading (HS6)	Database	Value (CFAF)	Quantity (kilograms)	Value density (CFAF/kilogram)	Duty (%)	Threshold value
O1	Cameroon Customs	203,847,479	514,810	396	10	No
	UN Comtrade	0 exportation	n.a.	n.a.	n.a.	n.a.
O2	Cameroon Customs	46,683,942	16,250	2,873	30	No
	UN Comtrade	36,629,504	15,000	2,500	n.a.	n.a.
O3	Cameroon Customs	366,152,535	250,227	1,463	30	Yes
	UN Comtrade	253,651,176	353,409	718	n.a.	n.a.
O4	Cameroon Customs	31,010,919	18,197	1,704	30	Yes
	UN Comtrade	9,592,128	11,346	845	n.a.	n.a.
O5	Cameroon Customs	238,418,743	116,575	2,045	30	No
	Comtrade	336,120,736	175,600	1,914	n.a.	n.a.
O6	Cameroon Customs	59,914,679	47,721	1,256	30	No
	UN Comtrade	13,716,704	11,904	1,152	n.a.	n.a.
O7	Cameroon Customs	13,755,840,998	28,608,610	481	30	No
	UN Comtrade	7,753,856,888	19,670,320	394	n.a.	n.a.
O8	Cameroon Customs	576,885,075	656,350	879	30	Yes
	UN Comtrade	2,357,264,480	5,659,690	417	n.a.	n.a.
O9	Cameroon Customs	809,076	529	1,529	30	No
	UN Comtrade	17,590,936	23,247	757	n.a.	n.a.
O10	Cameroon Customs	183,435,157	153,535	1,195	30	No
	UN Comtrade	129,423,456	203,934	635	n.a.	n.a.
O12	Cameroon Customs	9,888,492	10,871	910	30	No
	UN Comtrade	216,215,720	307,109	704	n.a.	n.a.

(continued next page)

Table 6A.1 *(continued)*

Subheading (HS6)	Database	Value (CFAF)	Quantity (kilograms)	Value density (CFAF/kilogram)	Duty (%)	Threshold value
O13	Cameroon Customs	5,524,621	3,673	1,504	30	Yes
	UN Comtrade	1,443,992	2,045	706	n.a.	n.a.
O14	Cameroon Customs	13,982,280	20,880	670	10	No
	UN Comtrade	11,949,656	15,960	749	n.a.	n.a.
O15	Cameroon Customs	14,490,949	20,118	720	30	No
	UN Comtrade	3,091,480	3,440	899	n.a.	n.a.
O16	Cameroon Customs	114,495,431	65,978	1,735	30	Yes
	UN Comtrade	2,447,228,744	3,640,151	672	n.a.	n.a.
O17	Cameroon Customs	8,777,230	5,409	1,623	30	No
	UN Comtrade	165,242,656	248,423	665	n.a.	n.a.
O18	Cameroon Customs	2,581,666,700	5,566,255	464	30	No
	UN Comtrade	179,319,992	5,560,683	32	n.a.	n.a.

Source: World Bank.
Note: n.a. = not applicable.

Notes

1. In special cases, such as that of the Democratic People's Republic of Korea, mirror statistics were used to fill a gap in published statistics. This use is, however, marginal. Most articles use mirror statistics to try to explain statistical discrepancies.

2. It confirms what Yeats (1978, 355) found: "Normal c.i.f.-f.o.b. ratios do not approximate transport costs in spite of the assumption often made in gravity flow and related trade models."

3. The units and extent of reporting depend on individual countries. Overall, quantity information in kilograms is provided for products that represent about 70 percent of value in the customs database.

4. Database coverage is not universal. Some countries do not report to UN Comtrade (for example, Algeria, the Islamic Republic of Iran, Iraq, and the Syrian Arab Republic), and other countries report to UN Comtrade, but their reporting is incomplete (for example, the United Arab Emirates reported data only in 2009 and Nigeria only in 2009 and 2010) or delayed (data from Brazil for 2007 and from the Netherlands for 2010 are not available). As a result, matching total import flows for all countries is not possible because of different country coverage (with the customs database being more comprehensive). Even when imports and exports can be matched, gaps in some years may remain (as in the case of Brazil and the Netherlands).

5. Significant individual differences occur for some of the 27 countries that belong to the EU because goods are shipped from a country different from the one in which they originated. In the remainder of this chapter, we treat the EU-27 as a group.

6. The original customs database contains information on imports for 2011. However, these observations were dropped from the analysis.

7. The number of countries drops from 203 to 176 after cleaning the list of erroneous entries and dropping entries from small islands and territories that do not belong to the World Bank's country classification.

References

Bhagwati, Jagdish. 1964. "On the Underinvoicing of Imports." *Bulletin of the Oxford University Institute of Economics and Statistics* 26 (4): 389–97.

———. 1967. "Fiscal Policies, the Faking of Foreign Trade Declarations, and the Balance of Payments." *Bulletin of the Oxford University Institute of Economics and Statistics* 29 (1): 61–77.

Fisman, Raymond, and Shang-Jin Wei. 2004. "Tax Rates and Tax Evasion: Evidence from 'Missing Imports' in China." *Journal of Political Economy* 112 (2): 471–96.

Javorcik, Beata S., and Gaia Narciso. 2007. "Differentiated Products and Evasion of Import Tariffs." Policy Research Working Paper 4123, World Bank, Washington, DC.

Kaminski, Bartłomiej, and Gaël Raballand. 2009. "Entrepôt for Chinese Consumer Goods in Central Asia: The Puzzle of Re-exports through Kyrgyz Bazaars." *Eurasian Geography and Economics* 50 (5): 581–90.

Pritchett, Lant, and Geetha Sethi. 1994. "Tariff Rates, Tariff Revenue, and Tariff Reform: Some New Facts." *World Bank Economic Review* 8 (1): 1–16.

Raballand, Gaël, and Edmond Mjekiqi. 2010. "Nigeria's Trade Policy Facilitates Unofficial Trade but Not Manufacturing." In *Putting Nigeria to Work*, ed. Volker Treichel, 203–28. Washington, DC: World Bank.

Rozanski, Jerzy, and Alexander Yeats. 1994. "On the (In)accuracy of Economic Observations: An Assessment of Trends in the Reliability of International Trade Statistics." *Journal of Development Economics* 44 (1): 103–30.

Yeats, Alexander. 1978. "On the Accuracy of Partner Country Trade Statistics." *Oxford Bulletin of Economics and Statistics* 40 (4): 341–61.

CHAPTER 7

Measuring Smuggling

Technical and Sociopolitical Issues: Algerian Customs as an Example

Hanane Benyagoub, Hakim Nait Abdelselam, and Aissa Boudergui

Smuggling is one of the oldest offenses that requires policing of customs borders (Becquet 1959). Although globalization and more sophisticated forms of fraud have substantially changed the legal notion of smuggling, the illegal movement of goods outside customs control posts continues to be a highly active and flexible operation. Smugglers are able immediately to exploit any shortcomings in border control mechanisms and can take advantage of the resource problems faced by the developing countries.

Africa is particularly vulnerable to this problem. With globalization, the continent has swiftly become a base for a whole range of operations: drug trafficking, illegal immigration, and smuggling. Growing trade and the development of international transport have made Africa, where police forces lack resources and public officials are badly paid, into an ideal hub for the concealment and transit of a wide range of illegal goods, including drugs, firearms, and resources with a high added value such as oil and timber. In a report published in June 2005, the United Nations Office on Drugs and Crime warned of the consequences of smuggling on

Africa's development and stressed that any informed study of this issue was hampered by the lack of statistical data (UNODC 2005).

Algeria is no stranger to this kind of fraud, which is growing apace. This chapter looks at the steps the Algerian customs administration has taken to combat smuggling by using quantification tools to improve the way in which smuggling is evaluated and policed. This quantitative approach has gradually highlighted the need for the administration to take a primarily analytical—but also global, social, and geographic—approach to the problem of smuggling, an approach that is not confined to university circles but that has to be implemented by administrations in partnership with universities.

The first section of the chapter looks at the legal, logistical, and human resources that have been deployed to combat smuggling and the way in which this resource deployment strategy was hampered early by the lack of a numerical culture that would have made it possible to evaluate how effective the system actually is. In the second section, the chapter looks at the introduction of a dedicated antismuggling and customs litigation information system designed to measure the problem and evaluate the effect of customs operations in the field in the best possible way. The chapter's conclusion is that this quantitative approach needs to be combined with qualitative approaches to take account of the socioeconomic circumstances surrounding smuggling and to consolidate and improve the response by customs administrations.

Smuggling: A Hidden Strategic Problem

In Algeria, offenses recorded outside customs posts and offices have been growing exponentially with the loss to the public exchequer rising from DA 18 billion in 2006 to over DA 61 billion (US$810 million) in 2011 (figure 7.1).

These overall figures highlight the increase in smuggling, but without a strong political resolve to step up the fight against smuggling, reflected recently by a tightening of legal provisions, few data are available on which to base an understanding of the problem.

The public authorities consider smuggling to be a threat to the country's security and stability[1] and have introduced new legal provisions. In 2005, a draft order presented by the minister for justice set out a specific and unprecedented criminal prosecution system.[2] This system includes preventive and organizational measures and criminal sanctions. Preventive measures include making Algeria's borders more secure, in particular in

Figure 7.1   Trends in Smuggling, by Value of Fines per Year, 2006–11

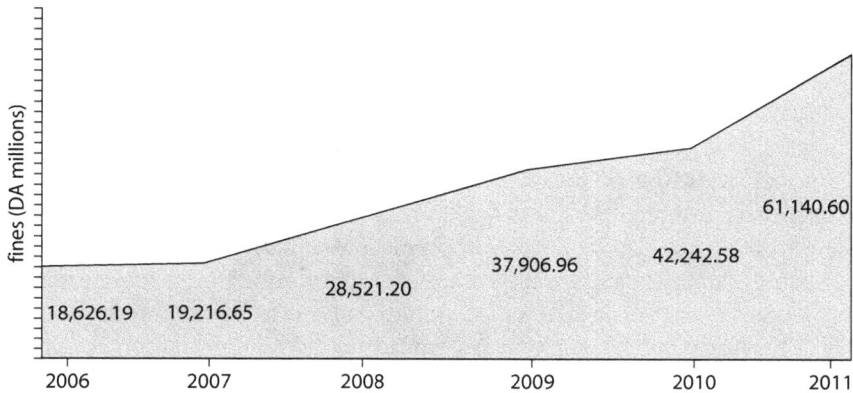

18,626.19   19,216.65   28,521.20   37,906.96   42,242.58   61,140.60

2006   2007   2008   2009   2010   2011

Source: General Directorate for Customs.

those areas remote from control sites, by stepping up the human and logistical resources of border security services; involving civil society through awareness-raising and information campaigns on the dangers of smuggling; making trade practices more ethical; and encouraging the reporting of smuggling operations and routes to the public authorities. In organizational terms, the investigative resources available to the forces of law and order have been stepped up (infiltration, controlled delivery, international cooperation), and under this new legislation, customs retains its twofold status as a service responsible for both investigation and law enforcement. Other security services must continue to hand over the procedure and any goods seized to the geographically competent customs receiver.[3] In terms of criminal sanctions, the order considers smuggling operations to be part of organized crime and gives them an unprecedented criminal dimension: prison terms may extend to life imprisonment for smuggling of firearms or smuggling that represents a threat to national security, the national economy, or public health.[4]

To optimize the application of the legislative system, the customs administration introduced a global strategy to combat smuggling by increasing human and logistical resources and setting up specialist training programs. Between 2006 and 2011, customs recruited 6,198 people, including 5,720 into the technical service; 40 percent of the operational staff attended specialist training, with 3,927 officers attending squad and antismuggling training; and customs logistical resources were stepped up—an equipment budget exceeding DA 2 billion was allocated to customs in 2010 (General Directorate for Customs 2012).

Although these initial measures allowed Algerian customs to undertake some highly significant one-off operations,[5] overall data that could serve as a basis for an informed debate about results have long been lacking. Algerian customs had no information system from which its action strategy could be synthesized and evaluated. Statistics on seizures and trends in intercepted fraud were regularly forwarded to the public authorities, but data collection took place manually. Although relatively reliable, this quantitative information was not enough, by its nature, to provide a basis for more detailed thinking about trends in fraud.

The lack of an information system through which this strategic action by the customs administration could be quantified also hampered evaluation of the efficiency of resources and operations in the field and checking of the relevance of the indicators set up to assess the performance of the operational units responsible for combating smuggling. The evaluation of measures to combat smuggling is part of a global performance system set up within the 2007–10 modernization program to enable the administration to move from a solely resource-based approach to a results-based approach. The General Directorate for Customs has drawn up the approach; the strategy to be followed; and the organization, management, and follow-up of the performance evaluation system of its decentralized external units.

In a first phase, mission letters detailing the action programs were sent to the regional directors (during the second half of 2008), paving the way for them to sign performance contracts for 2009. A first set of performance indicators was introduced, and permanent units (central and regional) were set up to ensure that the performance evaluation of external services was followed up.

The first performance contracts were signed by the director general and the regional directors in 2009 and then renewed in 2010. Version 1 of the performance indicators was introduced in 2009.[6] The list included a total of 21 indicators in three categories corresponding to the three main customs missions: fiscal issues (8 indicators), economic issues (2 indicators), and the fight against fraud and protection of the national and consumer economy (11 indicators). The provisions of the outline memorandum of May 5, 2009, and the outcome of the negotiation meetings held with regional and local officers in June and July 2009 provided a basis for tailoring the content of the indicators to the regional customs directorates to match the particular nature of their activities.

The 11 protection indicators (see table 7.1) are used to quantify anti-smuggling performance and are worded in a fairly similar way to the first generation of antismuggling indicators adopted by the French customs administration. Two indicators were omitted during this initial phase: the consumer protection indicator (P9) and the indicator of the number of networks dismantled (P10). The former indicator included all breaches of technical, health, and plant health standards. The calculation unit for the latter indicator included imprecise data (fraud sectors, large turnover) and a specific organizational criterion (interception of a minimum of three people belonging to the same group and playing a significant role in the network). The criteria were felt to be too vague or too complex for the measurement tools available to external units.

The calculation method for the protection indicators is based on the overall quantity of seizures made (numerator: total number of records, number of officers in post) or drawn up by categories of goods considered sensitive to smuggling (for example, narcotics, tobacco products, alcohol,

Table 7.1   Description of Protection Indicators by Objective and Calculation Method

Code	Indicator	Period (months)	Calculation method
P1	Efficiency ratio of seizures of narcotics by officer	3	Quantity of seizures/number of officers
P2	Efficiency ratio of seizures of tobacco products by officer	3	Quantity of seizures/number of officers
P3	Efficiency ratio of seizures of alcohol by officer	3	Quantity of seizures/number of officers
P4	Efficiency ratio of seizures of fuel by officer	3	Quantity of seizures/number of officers
P5	Efficiency ratio of seizures of livestock by officer	3	Livestock number/number of officers
P6	Amount of counterfeit seizures	3	Amount of counterfeit goods
P7	Amount of currencies and gold-bearing materials seized	3	Quantity of seizures/number of officers
P8	Number of arms seized	3	Quantity of seizures (by type of arms, explosives)
P11	Average reports by customs officer	3	Number of reports/number of agents

Source: General Directorate for Customs, memorandum 707/DGD/SP/DE.400/09 of May 5, 2009, on the establishment of the evaluation of the performance of external services.

fuel, livestock, counterfeit goods, currencies and gold-bearing materials, firearms).

The indicator's measurement unit is calculated quarterly and annually by the divisional inspectorate and the regional directorate and approved nationally. The performance thresholds are decided in line with the goals negotiated with the regional directors in terms of each region's specific mission focus and geographic location.

Efforts to steer the implementation of the antismuggling performance contracts nevertheless came up against a major obstacle: the lack of an information system when setting up the evaluation system. This gap tended to detract from the measurement because reliable data could not be immediately obtained. The results forwarded by the regional directorates were inconsistent and prevented the permanent central cell from mining and analyzing the data to help develop the system.

The Contribution of Information and Communication Technologies in Combating Smuggling and the Introduction of a Dedicated Customs Litigation Information System

In late 2009, the customs administration launched a study to design the Information System to Manage Customs Litigation (Système d'Information de Gestion du Contentieux Douanier, or SIGCD) to follow up its strategic work (investigations, legal proceedings, transaction procedures, recovery, breakdowns of revenue from fines and confiscation) beyond the customs clearance measures and procedures covered by the Automated Customs Management Information System (Système Informatique de Gestion Automatisé des Douanes, or SIGAD), which was introduced in 1995.[7]

The test version of SIGCD was installed in late 2010 in all the regional customs directorates. This version covers more than 17 of the 49 divisions, accounting for 71 percent of litigation. For test purposes, the regional directors were asked to input all litigation procedures in the last half of 2010 and to train and familiarize officers with this new tool and to propose any changes. In February 2011, version 1 was launched to include cases recorded during that year. In December 2011, the General Directorate for Customs had an online database containing more than 23,000 litigation files drawn up by customs units and the other security services authorized to report customs offenses. The total value of the litigation recorded in the system was over DA 91 billion (US$1.22 billion), corresponding to 18 percent of customs revenue (excluding hydrocarbons) for 2010.

SIGCD is in Arabic, which is Algeria's official language. The system is designed in Web mode on the customs administration private network and connects the services involved in litigation procedures within the same customs office (squads, antifraud services, litigation revenue) horizontally in real time, as well as providing a vertical real-time connection (office, regional directorate, central directorate).[8]

Each customs officer involved in the litigation procedure inputs the data from his work into the system. The seizure procedures undertaken by the security services are input by the customs receiver into SIGCD, indicating the status of the reporting service. This method allows the customs administration to centralize all antismuggling data. These data are made available to the local and central customs officers, who can monitor the work of their services online and compare it with the results of other services working to combat smuggling. The system swiftly proved to be a crucial development for sites not covered by SIGAD and undertaking only antismuggling work, because it allowed them to quantify their activities.

Although obvious benefits accrue from the point of view of transparency and visibility, installing a new information and measurement system in a public institution is not necessarily easy. The project came up against two main obstacles. The private customs network on which SIGCD is installed does not cover all services because areas are so large and some operational sites, largely at borders, are very remote. The current rate of coverage is 48 percent, and an extension project is currently under way. This technical problem has been used as an argument to call into question the advisability of the project and its efficiency. The human dimension of resistance to information and communication technologies is a real problem, and the systematic use of information within an administrative body may well be a source of major tensions and resistance because some perceive it as generating a power issue[9] and others as creating an additional workload.

Some results are nevertheless encouraging and open up interesting paths for analysis. Designed at the outset as a means of managing and monitoring customs litigation activities, the scope of the system's application has broadened beyond performance quantification, becoming a decision-making and resource allocation support tool.

Initial Qualitative Development: A Performance Evaluation Tool
To ensure ownership of SIGCD by the external services and to overcome their resistance, the system had to include a strong incentive to carry out performance measurement.

The fiscal and protection indicators whose data can be extracted directly from the system have been automated to ensure that the number production process is credible. These data are input by the customs officers involved in investigating the offense, judicial proceedings, and recovery procedures and are automatically fed into the indicator. This method means the result is reliable, although systematic checking of data continues to be necessary at this stage of the project.

The evaluation system has been improved by means of an interface providing operational units and their hierarchical superiors with real-time information on the proportion of seizures carried out, legal decisions in favor of the customs administration, and the level of collection of penalties in comparison with the objectives to be achieved. A method was set up to display and share data and thereby to integrate a numerical culture into customs services and thus provide a new management dynamic. The system enables customs services to compare their results with one another and with other policing services working in the same area.

Last, the connection with the legal information system, which is currently being set up, will pave the way for more reactive handling of litigation cases and will make information more reliable as a result of analysis methods comparing the data available to the courts on the same customs cases.

Second Qualitative Development: Better Allocation of Resources

The allocation of human resources in the squad-based regional directorates (which carry out only antismuggling work) follows a simple logic: increasing operational services to provide better coverage on the ground. As a percentage, some 88 percent of staff members are in investigation services, 7 percent in legal prosecution services, and 5 percent in recovery.[10]

By analyzing the data collected by the system, the director general can then decide where and in which units staff numbers need to be increased. This function is particularly important in the present context in which customs staff numbers are being substantially increased (6,198 people added between 2006 and 2011).

Third Qualitative Development: Files That Are Better Produced and Followed Up

The system also makes it possible to offset partially the lack of staff in litigation services responsible for legal prosecution and recovery. This lack of staff in the services handling litigation had been making control measures and reporting of offenses less effective, because no rigorous follow-up of the subsequent phases that are crucial in the success of such action was done.

Because customs litigation is, for the most part, a criminal procedure, it is highly circumscribed from the legal point of view, and some measures have to be scrupulously respected if proceedings are not to be dismissed. These services have faced a twofold problem. First, the growth of smuggling, the ban on the use of customs transactions, and the increase in the monetary penalties for this type of offense have substantially increased the workload of officers in the field and those responsible for legal prosecution and recovery. Second, management remains entirely manual and out of kilter with this new workload.

The immediate adverse impact was an increase in the number of files deemed inadmissible by the courts because they contained formal errors or were time barred, because they failed to comply with the essential requirements in records of seizures, and because of failure to lodge other legal acts or legal appeals within the required deadlines.[11]

To support the work of officers in the field, two functions were included in SIGCD: (a) some measures were automated to reduce human intervention, and (b) a warning system was set up to target internal control and optimize its effect by making it more proactive.

The system includes 18 automated legal documents (records, legal documents, recovery procedures) drawn up by lawyers from the central litigation department in accordance with the legal provisions in force. Only information about the interception (names and details of the persons intercepted, place, date and time of the record, description of the goods and resources subject to fraud, and the value of such goods) is added by the investigating officer. Penalties are automatically calculated (fines, confiscations, and countervalues of goods evading seizure), depending on the legal classification of the offense, the reliability of which is examined through the system's analysis of the concordance of certain data.

The system automatically calculates the breakdown of the amounts recovered (fines, proceeds from the sale of seized goods) in accordance with the percentages set out in the regulations in force. The automation of management procedures not only helps substantially improve management quality but also gives customs officers an immediate overview of the effect of their performance on their direct interests and the financing of customs' social works.[12]

Internal control has been stepped up by an integrated warning system that allows the officer responsible for the file and his hierarchical superiors to carry out a preliminary check (six months after the inputting of the record or three days before the expiry of the appeal deadlines; this period is set in proportion to the deadlines for criminal matters: 10 days for appeal and opposition and eight for application for review).

SIGCD uses the same warning system to identify perishable goods seized by the external services; hence, the goods can be sold as soon as possible, and any deterioration can be avoided.[13] Requests for sale prior to judgment are generated automatically so that services can react swiftly and forward requests as soon as possible to the relevant legal authorities. Warnings take the form of a dialogue box that appears on the user's interface as soon as SIGCD is opened and refers to the list of pending cases. These tools allow the services to be more reactive while operating with the same number of staff members.

Initial Quantitative Results and Initial Questions
The test version of the information system was commissioned only in late 2010, and therefore only a year is available in which to assess its impact. The relevance of the initial version of the antismuggling performance indicators adopted can nevertheless already be seen in this period.

By way of initial results, the seizures by the customs services of some sensitive products, such as narcotics, exceeded the expectations set out in the performance contracts signed in 2009 and renewed thereafter (by 9 to 32 percent), and the number of seizures by officer has also increased (by 38 percent). The proportion of seizures made by customs services in comparison with the other security services is very positive in some regions, compared with the proportional numbers of staff in each sector. These initial data and their internal dissemination show the ownership of the performance system by customs services and an acceptance of management values and notions that had, up to then, been considered to be alien and not really feasible in Algeria. These results also show that customs services possess intelligence about their territories that enables them to adapt their control methods to the expectations of the General Directorate for Customs as set out in the performance contract.

Measuring performance is crucial in evaluating the efficiency of the customs services and the resources that need to be allocated to them to carry out their tasks. It is therefore normal for customs services' efforts to be focused on this benchmark, which is seen as a priority objective. Performance measurement has therefore helped bring about genuine changes in management culture and has promoted greater dynamism and even a degree of rivalry between operational services.

The pertinence of the antismuggling indicators adopted nevertheless comes up against some limits. First, performance measurement is based solely on the quantity of seizures made. Thus, priority is given to the quantity rather than the quality of seizures. The statistics bear this out: 81 percent of seizures involve goods whose value is less than DA 100,000. Analysis of the data also shows that 88 percent of people taken in for questioning are acting alone, and 75 percent are not residents of the region. Seizures may be focused on easily identifiable targets that do not require sophisticated control mechanisms. In almost 24 percent of cases, fraudsters are not identified, and 83 percent of the people intercepted are unemployed, making less likely the collection of the very high legal penalties due to the public exchequer.

Second, the indicators are geared to what is visible—that is, what customs services know about and intercept (narcotics, arms, cigarettes, fuel)—and not to the reality of smuggling that, in principle, involves a wider range of products. The indicators are drawn up on the basis of the fraudulent movements known to customs services and to which they rightly have to respond and achieve conclusive results, the essential goal being security. As a result, the indicators may ensnare the control method in a vicious circle: performance is always based on the same type of goods. In these circumstances, the risk is therefore that performance measurement will shape and condition the control system in the field.

By way of example, customs launched a dialogue in 2011 with economic operators involved in foreign trade. At these interviews, some exporters alerted customs to major smuggling operations prejudicial to their activity. This information was backed up by figures showing that exports of agrifoodstuff products of Algerian origin to neighboring countries were growing, but the statistics were not reflecting these quantities of imports from Algeria. In the view of the operators, the difference could be attributed to the quantities of exports smuggled out. This kind of smuggling does not appear in the statistics, however, and customs services have little awareness of it.

The logic on which the indicators are based is not always in line with the logic of smuggling. Smuggling does not concentrate exclusively on a particular type of goods. Like any illegal commercial transaction, smuggling is driven by a risk-profit ratio. Any change in the control system and any price difference brought about by a fiscal or commercial decision in a neighboring country may give rise to, worsen, or reverse a form of smuggling or cause it to disappear.

The socioeconomic foundations of smuggling are complex and highly interwoven with informal trade (UNECA 1998). Smuggling takes many forms, not all of which have the same economic impact and security implications for the state. Smuggling may be limited to locally available goods and products for immediate consumption by border populations; it may be wider ranging and involve manufactured products for urban areas that are farther away; or it may pose a particular threat to national security, as in the case of drug trafficking or trafficking in firearms.

Individuals and groups carrying out smuggling do not always behave in the same way. Their form and scale differ in the same way as their abilities and areas of specialization. They operate in geographically different regions and use a wide range of tactics and mechanisms to circumvent the rules and avoid being caught. All these factors have to be taken into account if performance is to be improved, because one must understand how smuggling comes about and how it is structured. Rethinking our analysis methods is the first step.

The performance indicators are good in that they improve customs performance from a management viewpoint, but at the same time they deprive customs of its ability to anticipate what it needs if its action in the field is to be effective.

Beyond Administrative Reform: The Need for a Coherent and Global Response to Smuggling

To meet this objective, Algerian customs has launched a global and analytical strategy to understand smuggling and adapt the way in which customs responds to it. This strategy is based on new measurement techniques that are part of the information system previously described, as well as more qualitative approaches.

Crime Mapping, or the Spatial Analysis of Smuggling

Crime mapping, or the spatial analysis of crime, includes all research and analysis activities that take the geographic references of crimes and the places of residence of alleged offenders and victims as its basic data (Beauregard 2004). This working method has given rise to the science of geocriminology, or environmental criminology, widely used by U.S. and Canadian police (Savoie 2005). Crime mapping offers a visual representation of the concentration of crime (hot spots) and its features (Besson 2004) and may be a valuable tool in drawing up and implementing strategies to combat smuggling.

A pilot project for the geocoding of smuggling data is currently being studied. A major challenge has to be resolved before this coding is feasible: how to identify locations in the remote and nonurban regions preferred by smugglers. Global positioning systems seem to offer the best solution when addresses may not be available. At present, the addresses of offenses forwarded by the litigation management system are processed and converted into geographic coordinates to include this information.

Using a geographic information system, geocriminology or the geocoding of smuggling should help provide answers to the following types of questions:

- Why is smuggling concentrated in a particular spatial area?
- Why do smugglers choose this location rather than others?
- How can geographic shifts in some types of smuggling be explained?
- Have solutions to a type of smuggling in a particular place had the expected effects?

Geocoded data allow better understanding and monitoring of the development of smuggling in small or large geographic regions and exploration of the potential risks and protection factors specific to those areas. Precisely locating smuggling hot spots will help customs services carry out targeted surveillance, known as *precision surveillance*, rather than conventional monitoring by random patrols.

The purpose of this approach is to supplement the management strategy that has been in place since 2009 with a proactive and intelligent spatial approach through which smuggling flows can be anticipated. Moreover, the existence of performance indicators and an information system that collects data and generates them automatically will help with the quantitative evaluation of the effects of these tools and their level of ownership by the operational services.

Toward a Global Approach to Illegal Acts

Smuggling is a multidimensional security, economic, and social problem, and customs administrations therefore have to equip themselves with tools to make it more visible and gain a better understanding of the problem. To include this concern in its reform, the customs administration is implementing an administrative strategy as yet unparalleled in most sectors of the Algerian civil service: scientific cooperation with universities, in the form of a mixed research unit, to pinpoint and draw up guidelines for the prevention of smuggling from the quantitative data generated by the customs administration. This initiative combines the concerns of both researchers, to whom little quantitative information on crime is usually available (because such information, when it exists, is kept by government agencies), and the customs administration, which, beyond its law enforcement mission, possesses resources able to inform its policy on and response to crime in terms of enforcement and prevention.

It should be stressed that the Algerian government is encouraging the creation of research units within the public administration.[14] These developments in state administration techniques and the concerns of some university circles have made it possible to draw up a notion of applied science able to satisfy the requirements of both the customs administration and researchers for the public good. This cooperation led to the conclusion, in March 2011, of a partnership between the Algerian customs administration and the Applied Development Economics Research Centre (Centre de Recherche en Économie Appliqué pour le Développement, or CREAD) within a national research program funded by the government.[15]

Ownership of the Tools of Applied Criminology

Effectively combating smuggling makes it necessary not just to quantify volumes of smuggling but also to understand the behavior of the individuals and groups undertaking this kind of illegal activity. This vision goes beyond information methods and requires a global understanding that can be achieved by using the tools of applied criminology (Szabo 1978).

The cooperation between the customs administration and CREAD within a mixed unit is intended to find answers to three main questions:

- How and why is smuggling increasing and cross-border trade becoming more instrumental?
- How should criminological profiling be structured?
- How are groups structured and how do they develop?

This last question encompasses issues such as impulsive and intermittent individual activity, temporary and loosely structured groups, more structured groups trading in influence, bribery, and integration into international trade circuits.

Criminal profiling optimizes the management efficiency targeted by the administrative reform policy by highlighting what works at particular times and in particular places and what is best at the least cost for the state (the cost-benefit ratio).

Integration of the Socioeconomic Dimension into the Antismuggling System

The political authority ensures that laws and the structures responsible for enforcing them are in keeping with the constantly changing reality of society and its tolerance of illegal activities and law enforcement systems. The current legislation governing cross-border trade can be analyzed from the point of view of its acceptance by the people it targets, the populations living in those areas, and the economic operators working with or in those areas. This approach is what is known in the English-speaking world as *compliance*—that is, the spontaneous respect for the law by users, which works only if users are highly involved in deciding on the rule of law (Mandelkern 2005).

Preventing crime means adapting social relations. Applied research will allow assessment of the existing legislation and pinpoint potential options not requiring fresh legal rules by reexamining what already exists, what needs to be modified, what needs to be repealed, and what new rules need to be introduced. The contribution from social disciplines will reduce the substantial information gap between those who decide on change (government officials and senior administrators), those who implement it (officials in the field), and those who are subject to it (the people). This increased information should ultimately make possible the addition of a social element to the legal approach.

The partnership between the customs administration and CREAD supports this vision. As part of the research program to improve the quality of services for users, research into informal trade is one of the main aspects to be studied.

Conclusion

The economic and security issues surrounding smuggling mean that the customs administration must achieve results and demonstrate that it is providing a proper response. Methods have been introduced to evaluate the consequences and the precise scope of each customs operation (checks, investigations, legal proceedings, enforcement of fiscal penalties) as it takes place. Quantification systems are currently in place, and some instruments of criminology, such as crime mapping of smuggling, are being envisaged. Using quantification for management and organizational purposes helps reallocate resources, make customs services more proactive, and provide customs officers with better training in geographic intelligence.

Although these tools may help improve performance, some doubts persist about their reliability, because they do not measure smuggling but rather the reaction of the customs services to this form of fraud. The tools need to be consolidated by including criminological analysis and a better understanding of the socioeconomic environment. The customs administration is using this new approach by including scientific research in its reform strategy.

Notes

1. See, for example, the statement made by the minister for justice (in *Official Journal of Debates* 10, 2005) when presenting the draft order on combating smuggling to the Senate.

2. See Order 05-06 of 18 Rajab 1426, corresponding to August 23, 2005, on combating smuggling. The order was approved by Law 05-17 of 29 Dhou el Kaada 1426, corresponding to December 31, 2005. This order repeals and replaces the criminal provisions on smuggling set out in the Algerian Customs Code under articles 326, 327, and 328.

3. Article 244 of the Algerian Customs Code remains in force under Order 05-06 on combating smuggling.

4. See articles 14 and 15 of Order 05-06. The public authorities repealed the criminal provisions set out in the Customs Code (articles 326, 327, and 328) and replaced them with more severe penalties. The maximum prison terms set out in other articles were increased from 5 years to 20 years, and fines were increased from a maximum penalty of 4 to 10 times the overall value of the smuggled goods and resources. The order also prohibits any customs transaction in this type of offense (article 21 of Order 05-06).

5. For instance, on December 21, 2008, the customs services in Tébessa (eastern borders) seized over €3 million in cash. The customs services in El Taref (eastern borders) seized €1 billion on June 9, 2009, and the customs services in Béchar (western borders) seized over three metric tons of drugs on October 29, 2009.

6. See the May 5, 2009, memorandum from the director general of customs (707/DGD/SP/DE.400/09).

7. SIGAD handles the customs clearance procedure and covers 96.78 percent of customs sites controlling commercial operations.

8. SIGCD is based on a 3-tier architecture and uses the customs intranet. Data centralization is performed by dedicated servers on two levels, regional (regional management) and national (headquarters).

9. Some studies on the use of the information and communication technologies in public security services show the problems raised by the introduction of new information tools in these services (see, for instance, Ratcliffe 2000).

10. These statistics from 2011 are based on the average allocation of two regional directorates largely undertaking antismuggling tasks.

11. Ministry of Justice statistics were not available at the time of writing of this chapter.

12. In accordance with the regulations in force, 30 percent of the proceeds of fines and confiscations go to the customs mutual association, social works, and the customs orphans' fund.

13. SIGCD lists 1,754 goods in 2011 that must be sold prior to judgment.

14. See Decree 99-257 of November 16, 1999, on the creation, organization, and operation of a research unit.

15. See Law of February 23, 2008, setting out guidelines and a five-year scientific research and technological development program for 2008–12.

References

Beauregard, Éric. 2004. "La géocriminologie." In *Dictionnaire des sciences criminelles*, ed. Gérard Lopez and Stamatios Tzitzis, 450–52. Paris: Editions Dalloz.

Becquet, Paul. 1959. *La contrebande: Législation, jurisprudence, usages et pratiques de la douane*. Paris: Librairies techniques.

Besson, Jean-Luc. 2004. *Les cartes du crime*. Paris: Presses Universitaires de France.

General Directorate for Customs. 2012. *Bilan de modernisation de l'administration des douanes 2007–2010*. Algiers: General Directorate for Customs.

Mandelkern, Dieudonné. 2005. *La qualité de la réglementation*. Paris: La Documentation.

Ratcliffe, Jerry H. 2000. "Implementing and Integrating Crime Mapping into a Police Intelligence Environment." *International Journal of Police Science and Management* 2 (4): 313–23.

Savoie, Josée. 2005. "Le géocodage des données de la criminalité: Étude de faisabilité de recueillir des données auprès des services de police." Centre Canadien de la Statistique Juridique, Statistique Canada, Ottawa.

Szabo, Denis. 1978. *Criminologie et politique criminelle*. Paris: Librairie Philosophique.

UNECA (United Nations Economic Commission for Africa). 1998. "Les inci-
    dences économiques du commerce informel frontalier." Document ECA/
    SRDC-CA/TC/98/03, Centre de Développement Sous-Régional pour
    l'Afrique Centrale, UNECA, Addis Ababa.

UNODC (United Nations Office on Drugs and Crime). 2005. *Crime and
    Development in Africa.* Geneva: UNODC.

CHAPTER 8

Measuring the Effects of the Republic of Korea's Single Window System

Soyoung Yang

Overcoming inefficiencies in border procedures continues to be a key objective of both governments and the private sector. Regulatory requirements that are duplicative are a significant encumbrance on trade (Mustra 2011). For instance, in many countries, traders must submit transaction information to several border agencies as part of the border formalities process. This duplication is inefficient and adds to delays in cargo dwell times and transaction costs. Policy makers and traders have thus sought decreases in the labyrinth of cross-border trade processes through the creation of one information portal for all border agencies. Such systems would enable traders to submit required information only once to a government portal, which then transmits the data to all appropriate border agencies. This simple idea became the *single window* concept (UNECE 2011; WCO 2008). This chapter reviews the implementation, beginning in 2006, of a single window system by the Korea Customs Service (KCS) and the use of measurement to evaluate its effect.[1] Measurement shows that average clearance times for transactions that have to pass through customs and licensing agencies have decreased by one day. Moreover, by the fourth year of implementation, a cost-benefit analysis indicated that the Republic of Korea was able to recoup its investment in this trade facilitation reform.

Korea's Single Window System

The central motive for KCS's deployment of the single window was the fundamental focus of the Korean economy on international trade (see table 8.1). To that end, the Korean government has emphasized the efficiency of border controls, such as the automation of trade regulation processes.

Although Korea's international trade volumes continued to rise, border management costs did not decrease as much as planned. The government's analysis was that Korea should seek to reduce inefficiencies caused by the multiplicity of border agencies. Accordingly, the government found the concept of single window attractive because it might lead to harmonized development of the trade environment as a whole and improve the performance of border management relatively quickly at a reasonable cost. The KCS Management Planning Division created a task force that consisted of customs officers, business consultants, and software engineers to develop the single window system. KCS developed and implemented the system from 2004 to 2008 and invested KRW 67 billion (approximately US$5.4 million).[2] Most of the development work was completed in 2008, and since then KCS has focused on increasing the number of participating agencies.

Performance Measurement

To evaluate the effect of Korea's single window, one ideally would use a randomized controlled trial to reduce threats to validity (Shadish, Cook,

Table 8.1   Share of International Trade to Gross Domestic Product

	Share (%)								
	2000	2001	2002	2003	2004	2005	2006	2007	2008
Korea, Rep.	37.1	34.6	32.4	34.2	38.8	37.9	39.0	41.2	53.5
Total for Organisation for Economic Co-operation and Development members	22.2	21.7	21.5	22.1	23.6	24.7	26.4	27.5	28.9

Source: OECD 2011.

and Campbell 2002). KCS's single window was developed incrementally, however, and its development and implementation occurred nearly simultaneously. In other words, unlike a medicine waiting for evaluation after its development is completed, the single window was fully implemented at the same time as its development was completed. Traders were not keen to accept a discriminating environment in which some would be allowed to use the single window system and others would not simply to improve the validity of the research findings. In addition, KCS sought rapid and comprehensive implementation.

KCS's historical collection of data led to the possibility of conducting a performance evaluation after implementation. For instance, since the implementation of its automated clearance system in the late 1990s, KCS has regularly recorded elapsed time between the arrival of goods at ports and the release from customs control at each data entry point.[3] In particular, since the introduction of the balanced scorecard as a performance management tool in 2006 (Kaplan and Norton 1996), KCS has measured the performance of several processes (for example, cargo clearance, passenger clearance, postclearance audits, and investigation of smuggling).

On the basis of these conditions, KCS measured the time it took for clearance of goods for two groups submitting declarations and requiring license approvals. The first group consisted of declarations processed through the single window system, and the second group included declarations processed through customs and licensing agencies separately. During implementation, the size of group 1 increased and that of group 2 dwindled as more declarations were processed through the single window.

Reductions in Time for Clearance of Goods

Before implementation of the single window, clearing goods that required licenses, inspections, or approvals generally took more than four days: two to three days for the internal process of licensing agencies, one day for transferring decisions of licensing agencies to KCS, and one and one-half hours for customs clearance decisions (table 8.2). Previously, after submitting license applications, traders had to pick up the approval at a licensing agency and forward it to KCS for examination. The single window, however, automatically links a license to a customs declaration, which means that traders do not need to visit both licensing agencies and the customs office, thereby reducing the processing time by one day. Consequently, clearing goods that require licenses now takes approximately three days.

Table 8.2   Clearance Time Saved by the Single Window

	Issuance of license	Transferal of license to customs office	Acceptance of declaration
Before single window	2–3 days	1 day	1.5 hours
After single window	2–3 days	0	1.5 hours

Source: KCS.

Cost Reductions

KCS's single window reduced costs for traders in two ways. First, because of the one-stop system, traders saved transportation costs for moving between licensing and customs agencies. Second, several kinds of documents were no longer needed, which saved the costs incurred for preparing redundant paperwork. Moreover, the single window system enabled traders to save transaction fees that would otherwise have been charged by value-added network (VAN) service companies. The single window system was designed to operate using the Internet; before the introduction of single window, KCS transformed its VAN-based automated clearance system and discarded the old-fashioned VAN environment. The World Bank reported that the reform's overall cost savings reached US$2.1 billion annually (World Bank 2009).

Cost-Benefit Analysis

Many stakeholders believed that the single window would contribute to the reduction of transaction costs. To provide confirmation of this, KCS conducted a cost-benefit analysis on the single window system. The assumptions of the analysis were that the cost was the amount spent to develop and implement the system and that the benefit was the reduction in transaction costs achieved by simplifying the trade process and making relevant documents electronic. KCS has invested KRW 85.6 billion (approximately US$7.8 million) in the single window over nine years. The benefits are the direct cost savings measured by the reduction of data processing time and the elimination of the transaction fee charged by VAN companies.

According to a National Information Society Agency study (NIA 2006), traders who used to shuttle between customs and licensing saved about 100 minutes per declaration. Therefore, given the time saving per declaration (1.7 hours); the average wage per hour for an employee in a trading company (KRW 12,702, or approximately US$11.50); and the transaction fee per declaration charged by VAN companies (KRW 500, or approximately US$0.40), the direct benefit of the single window can be calculated as follows:

$$(\text{number of declarations} \times 1.7 \text{ hours})$$
$$\times \text{KRW } 12{,}702 + (\text{number of declarations} \times \text{KRW } 500).$$

Table 8.3 reflects cost savings under the single window: as the number of licensing agencies connected to the system increases, the number of declarations processed increases, thus leading to an increase in cost savings.

Figure 8.1 shows the accumulated costs and benefits since 2006. The cost-benefit analysis based on data from the figure indicates that the single window reached a break-even point in 2009 (the fourth year) and achieved benefits more than six times the system's investment in 2011.

Table 8.3   Direct Benefits from the Single Window

	2006	2007	2008	2009	2010	2011
Agencies connected to single window	8	11	11	15	17	31
Declarations	25,132	50,284	140,171	477,372	832,453	989,430
Cost saving (US$ million)	0.49	0.99	2.75	9.37	16.34	19.42
Accumulated benefit (US$ million)	0.49	1.48	4.23	13.60	29.95	49.37

Source: KCS.

Figure 8.1   Comparison between the Costs and Benefits of the Single Window, 2006–11

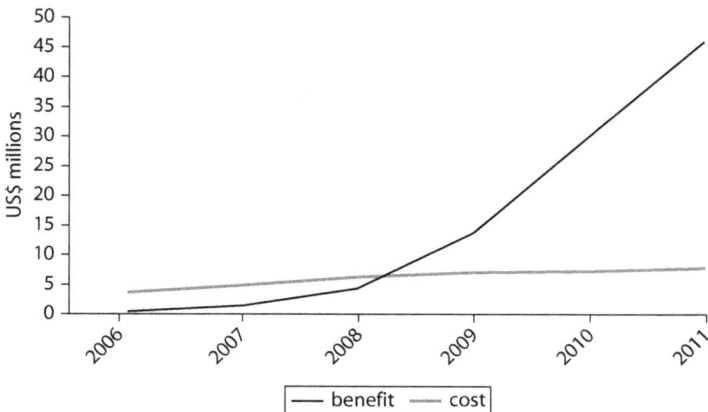

Source: KCS.

Conclusion

To improve trade facilitation, KCS established a single window system to streamline the border regulatory process. Measurement shows that for businesses submitting their required information, clearance time has been reduced by one day. In addition, a cost-benefit analysis shows that the investment was worth the return.

Annex 8A: KCS's Single Window Implementation Process

Early Stages

As a first step, KCS conducted business process reengineering (BPR) and information strategic planning (ISP) from November 2003 to June 2004. Because single window should cover all kinds of clearance-related processes, KCS needed to understand other trade-related agencies' business processes. KCS officers and business consultants carried out the BPR and ISP because it was thought that streamlining redundant processes would lead to stakeholder conflict.

Using a master plan, KCS invested KRW 2.6 billion (approximately US$2.4 million) to develop a single window prototype between August 2004 and March 2006 (table 8A.1). The focus was to shift trade documents from paper to electronic, provide traders with an environment that allowed them to submit all applications and declarations once, automatically distribute all applications and declarations to relevant agencies, and return agency responses to traders.

Initially, KCS introduced standardized electronic marine-air conveyance and passenger-crew list reports for processing in the single window. Airlines and shippers could thus submit reports once, whereas previously they submitted the same data separately to several agencies using slightly different formats. KCS then expanded single window to cover clearance processes and to connect KCS and eight major licensing agencies. From

Table 8A.1   Single Window Development Phases

Phase	Period	Development	Budget (US$ millions)
I	November 2003–June 2004	BPR and ISP carried out	0.1
II	August 2004–March 2006	Single window prototype developed	2.4
III	March 2006–February 2007	Agencies added to single window	1.3
IV	January 2008–July 2008	Reliability of single window improved	1.6

Source: KCS.

March 2006 to February 2007, three more organizations joined single window. KCS invested KRW 1.7 billion (approximately US$1.6 million) to improve reliability and provide a user-friendly environment for users from January to July 2008. After the development was completed through four phases, the list of agencies connected to the single window increased to include 11 out of 45 license agencies.

Single Window Composition

Experts categorize several types of single windows. The United Nations Center for Trade Facilitation and Electronic Business presents four single window reference models based on how information is collected and processed: single authority, automated information transaction system, integrated single automated system, and interfaced single automated system (UN 2005). Single window systems also can be classified into two types depending on coverage (Siva 2011). One is single window lite (SWL), which covers all import, export, and transit-related regulatory requirements. The other is trade facilitation single window (TFSW), which encompasses not only all import, export, and transit-related regulatory requirements but also commercial logistics requirements. In other words, SWL focuses on transactions between businesses and government, whereas TFSW handles business-to-business transactions regarding logistics as well as business-to-government transactions. Given the classifications, KCS's single window is regarded as an automated information transaction single window system and SWL, in that it was designed to concentrate on processing data that are supposed to be submitted to the customs administration.

Another perspective for examining single window systems focuses on users. The KCS's single window consists of two parts related to the type of user: (a) consolidation of conveyance reports, which addresses carrier concerns, and (b) linking of licenses and declarations, which is for traders.

Consolidation of conveyance reports. Airlines and shippers were required to submit their entry and departure reports and their officer and crew lists to border agencies when their aircraft or vessel arrived at or left a port. They submitted almost the same data, in only slightly different formats, to several border agencies, such as customs, immigration, quarantine, port authority, and aviation administration. Moreover, they had to pay a transaction fee to VAN companies mediating between airlines or shippers and border agencies whenever they sent their reports to each agency because border agencies did not share the reports with one another.

To solve this problem, KCS drew up a standardized format for conveyance reports and officer and crew lists to allow the single window to consolidate data from airlines and shippers (figure 8A.1). Airlines and shippers could then send their reports electronically to single window once, which then would automatically distribute the reports to several border agencies. Airlines and shippers thus benefited from reduced costs incurred to prepare duplicate reports.

Figure 8A.1   Consolidation of Conveyance Reports through the Single Window

a. Before single window

b. After single window

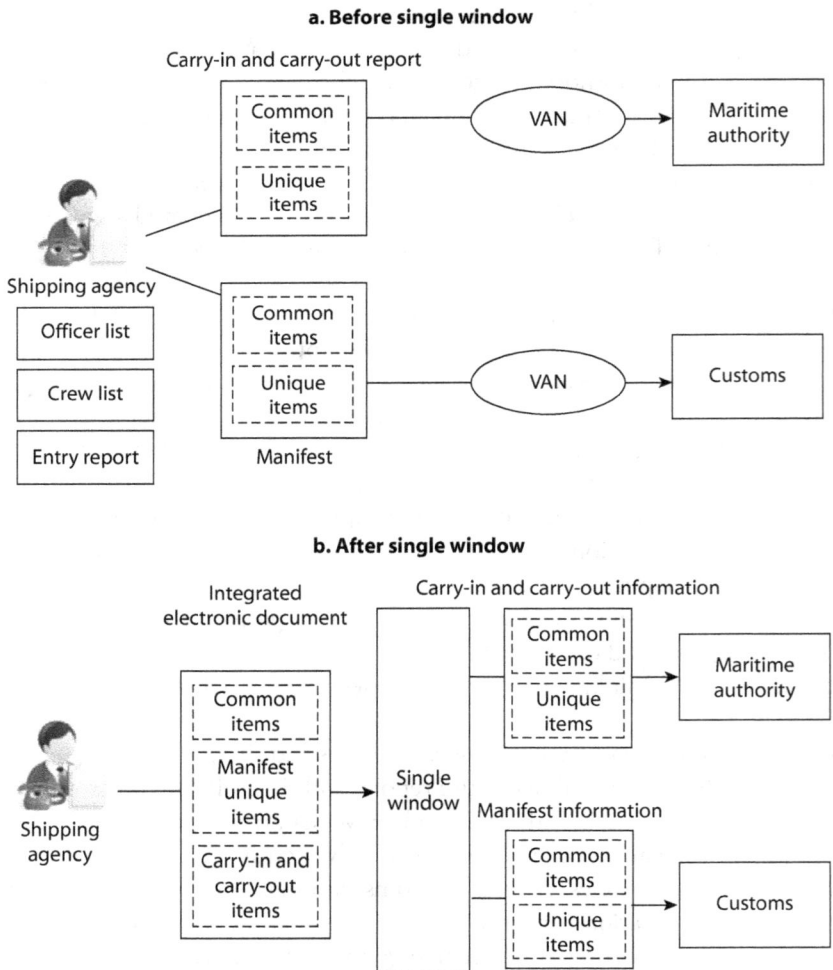

Source: KCS.
Note: VAN = value-added network.

Linking of licenses and approvals to declarations. The cross-border trade process involves a number of players. Exporters, importers, and financial institutions are involved at the stage of making contracts and payments. Freight forwarders, warehouses, airlines, and shippers carry out logistics. For clearance of goods at borders, a number of players also work together (Siva 2011). A mistaken belief in this case, however, was that the clearance process of imported and exported goods was done only by KCS. Although KCS plays a pivotal role in clearance, it is not the only player. Several licensing agencies clear types of goods that require special inspections or controls. Thus, to export and import such goods, traders had to deal not only with KCS but also with license agencies. The traders were required to submit declarations with licenses to KCS. Hence, to import and export, traders had to visit both licensing agencies and the customs office and to submit similar information.

The environment, however, changed after the introduction of single window, because it linked traders to customs and licensing agencies through the Internet (figure 8A.2). Traders no longer needed to physically visit licensing agencies and the customs office separately to submit their applications and declarations and to receive notification of agency decisions. Traders no longer needed to pay a transaction fee to VAN companies to submit their applications and declarations. The single window system enabled licensing agencies and KCS to exchange and share trader and goods information without intervention by traders.

The KCS single window was developed on top of the legacy systems of the licensing and customs agencies. In other words, it connects and respects legacy systems of these agencies. Thus, licensing agencies did not have to dismantle or give up their legacy systems to participate in single window; they merely needed to adjust their business procedures slightly.

Major Challenges
Several challenges were encountered in implementation of the system.

Low use rate. When the single window initiative was launched in 2006, the use rate was less than 3 percent. This problem was attributed to several factors. The single window at that time was not well known to stakeholders. In response, KCS provided an intensive training program for key stakeholders, such as customs brokers, to raise the rate of use. The number of participating agencies was also small. Some licensing agencies were

Figure 8A.2   Change in the Declaration Process through the Single Window

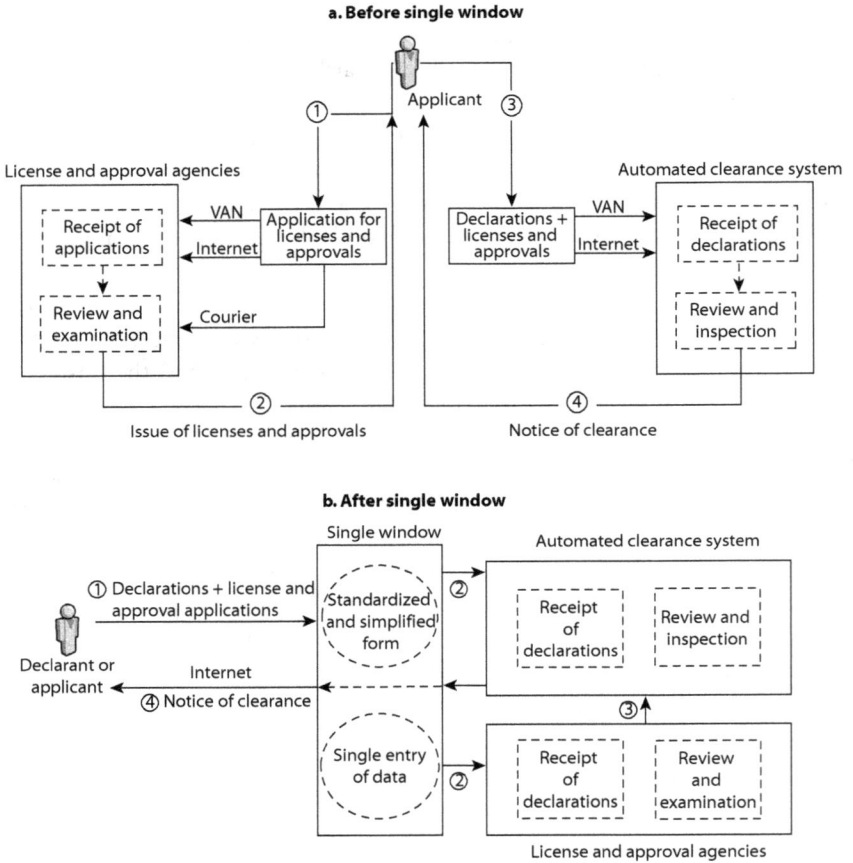

a. Before single window

Applicant

License and approval agencies

Receipt of applications

VAN ← Application for licenses and approvals
Internet →

Review and examination ← Courier

② Issue of licenses and approvals

Automated clearance system

Declarations + licenses and approvals

VAN → Receipt of declarations
Internet

Review and inspection

④ Notice of clearance

b. After single window

Single window

① Declarations + license and approval applications

Standardized and simplified form

Declarant or applicant ← Internet
④ Notice of clearance

Single entry of data

Automated clearance system

Receipt of declarations | Review and inspection ②

Receipt of declarations | Review and examination ③ ②

License and approval agencies

Source: KCS.
Note: VAN = value-added network.

reluctant to join because they feared that stakeholders might forget them. Some did not have their own automated license systems that they could connect to the single window. To help agencies that could not afford to develop their own stand-alone system into single window, KCS developed a special system that allowed automatic license operating on the single window. This system is called the application service providing (ASP) system. The ASP system provides small licensing agencies with the ability to process their licenses electronically. As of 2011, 10 agencies had their own license systems, which were directly linked to single window, and 21 agencies were using the ASP system. Accordingly, the ASP system contributed to the expanded coverage of the single window. Most of the remaining 14 nonparticipant agencies were local governments and local police agencies, which did not specialize in trade-related businesses. KCS is still endeavoring to encourage those agencies to join the single window through diverse incentives.

Coordination among related agencies. Compared to automated clearance systems, the single window system has been implemented in only a handful of countries. One might think that customs automation would follow a sequence: the introduction of the single window would be the final step to conduct after all trade-related agencies had finished developing their own automated systems. The KCS experience, however, shows a different story. Single window implementation is a political process. It was not demanding in terms of technology. Drawing various regulatory agencies under the umbrella of the single window, however, required a great deal of time, energy, and patience. In particular, agencies with their own well-developed systems were reluctant to participate because they believed that by joining they would lose their identity and their reason for existence. Thus, KCS designed the single window as an independent system that respected each agency's legacy system. KCS did not rush to increase the number of participating agencies. KCS let customers (for example, traders, freight forwarders, and customs brokers) who experienced advantages of the single window persuade nonparticipating agencies to join.

Enlistment of agencies in the single window system did not mean automatic completion; a challenging process still remained, which involved coordinating the related agencies. Many agencies had their own computerized systems and used different data formats for their own purposes. Even though implementation of a single window system does not require border and licensing agencies to demolish or merge their computerized systems, participating agencies had concerns about the survival of their systems. Such concerns arose because coordinating the related agencies' business processes and harmonizing their data formats was necessary. Thus, to address agencies' concerns about the single window, KCS and eight major border and licensing agencies formed a task force to coordinate each agency's business process and data format. The task force held more than 16 rounds of working-level meetings. As a result, the task force had many participating agencies consider the implications of the single window, which led to the revision of seven relevant laws and the modification of 10 application and declaration forms related to eight agencies (table 8A.2).

Table 8A.2 Data Harmonization in 10 Declaration Forms

Law		Required document	Total number of elements	Number of common elements	Number of noncommon elements	Elements eliminated
Livestock Products Processing Act		Livestock products import declaration	55	27 (49%)	14	14
Act on Prevention of Livestock Epidemics		Animal quarantine application	23	16 (70%)	4	3
		Livestock quarantine application	25	19 (76%)	4	2
Plant Protection Act		Plant inspection application	52	21 (40%)	11	20
Food Sanitation Act	Nonmarine food products	Food products import declaration	93	22 (24%)	30	41
	Marine products	Food products import declaration	79	24 (30%)	16	39
Pharmaceutical Affairs Act		Standard clearance schedule report	88	22 (25%)	13	53
Medical Device Act	General	Standard clearance schedule report	51	15 (29%)	9	75
	Dental	Standard clearance schedule report	51	15 (29%)	9	75
Pharmaceutical Affairs Act (for Animals)		Standard clearance schedule report	28	19 (68%)	1	8
Totals (for seven acts)		10	542	185 (34%)	102	255 (47%)

Source: KCS.

Notes

1. More information on the implementation process is presented in annex 8A.
2. This study used the exchange rate US$1 equals KRW 1,100.
3. The initial value-added, network-based automated clearance system was transformed to the web-based system called Uni-Pass in 2005.

References

Kaplan, Robert S., and David P. Norton. 1996. "Using the Balanced Scorecard as a Strategic Management System." *Harvard Business Review* 74 (1): 75–85.

Mustra, Monica A. 2011. "Border Management Modernization and the Trade Supply Chain." In *Border Management Modernization*, ed. Gerard McLinden, Enrique Fanta, Davide Widdowson, and Tom Doyle, 23–35. Washington, DC: World Bank.

NIA (National Information Society Agency). 2006. *Performance Measurement of Informatization of Korea Customs Service and Development of Performance Measurement Model* [in Korean]. Seoul: NIA.

OECD (Organisation for Economic Co-operation and Development). 2011. *OECD Factbook 2010–2011: Economic, Environmental, and Social Statistics.* Paris: OECD.

Shadish, William, Thomas Cook, and Donald Campbell. 2002. *Experimental and Quasi-Experimental Designs for Generalized Causal Inference.* Boston: Houghton Mifflin.

Siva, Ramesh. 2011. "Developing a National Single Window: Implementation Issues and Considerations." In *Border Management Modernization*, ed. Gerard McLinden, Enrique Fanta, Davide Widdowson, and Tom Doyle, 125–46. Washington, DC: World Bank.

UN (United Nations). 2005. "Recommendation and Guidelines on Establishing a Single Window: To Enhance the Efficient Exchange of Information between Trade and Government." United Nations Center for Trade Facilitation and Electronic Business Recommendation 33, United Nations, Geneva.

UNECE (United Nations Economic Commission for Europe). 2011. *Single Window Implementation Framework.* Geneva: United Nations.

World Bank. 2009. *Doing Business 2010: Reforming through Difficult Times.* Washington, DC: World Bank.

WCO (World Customs Organization). 2008. "Single Window: Implications for Customs Administrations." WCO, Brussels. http://www.wcoomd.org/files/6. SW_Files/SW%20Initiatives/WCO/003-Implications.pdf.

www.ingramcontent.com/pod-product-compliance
Lightning Source LLC
Chambersburg PA
CBHW061742270326
41928CB00011B/2339